I0202959

The Story of the
2/1st Wessex Field Ambulance

1914 - 1919.

The Naval & Military Press Ltd

Published by

The Naval & Military Press Ltd

Unit 5 Riverside, Brambleside
Bellbrook Industrial Estate
Uckfield, East Sussex
TN22 1QQ England

Tel: +44 (0)1825 749494

www.naval-military-press.com
www.nmarchive.com

*In reprinting in facsimile from the original, any imperfections are inevitably reproduced
and the quality may fall short of modern type and cartographic standards.*

Contents.

List of Illustrations.

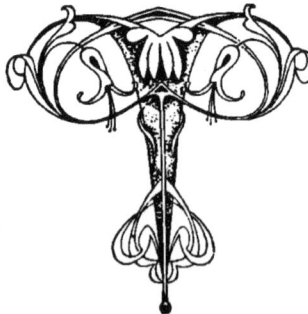

Lieut.-Col. W. Blackwood, D.S.O.,
Officer Commanding from July, 1917, to the termination
of Hostilities, November, 1918.

Foreword.

Of books about the War there will, I suppose, be a never-ending stream. Histories, chronicles, diaries, theories "about it and about," novels, poems—in fact, every conceivable thing which may be set up in type, and which has some bearing on the titanic struggle will pour from the publishers all over the world.

Yet we hope and believe that there is a little place somewhere for "The Story of the 2/1st Wessex Field Ambulance."

Those who were proud to belong to "our mob," and who shared its ups and downs, its good times and its bad, treasure many a memory which time will never efface. We know that as we were a "second-line." the Unit will not continue indefinitely, that there will come a time when the good old "Second-First" will be no more. Yet our memories of "the crowd" will last us all our lives.

It is, then, with the hope that this book will serve as a treasured souvenir, bringing back thoughts which maybe have grown dim, reminding us of the days when we lived and worked together as **men**, that we, with something of confidence, send out our little volume on its mission.

Our readers will know that between the covers will be found the work of many pens. We thank all our contributors ; and at the same time would like to mention the great help given by Lieut.-Col. W. Blackwood, D.S.O., Sergts. G. E. Essex and F. H. Salter, and Cpl. J. A. Lockton, while many thanks are due to Cpl. H. Constance (late of 24th Field Ambulance), who assisted in getting our book ready for the printers, and who kindly corrected the proofs.

Unfortunately it was found impossible to include all of the large number of contributions which were sent, so those responsible for this volume have, after careful consideration, made as wide a selection as possible.

In conclusion, we wish all "Wessex Boys" the best of luck and health now that their work in the War is done.

THE EDITOR,
SERGT. W. PEARCE, D.C.M., M.M.

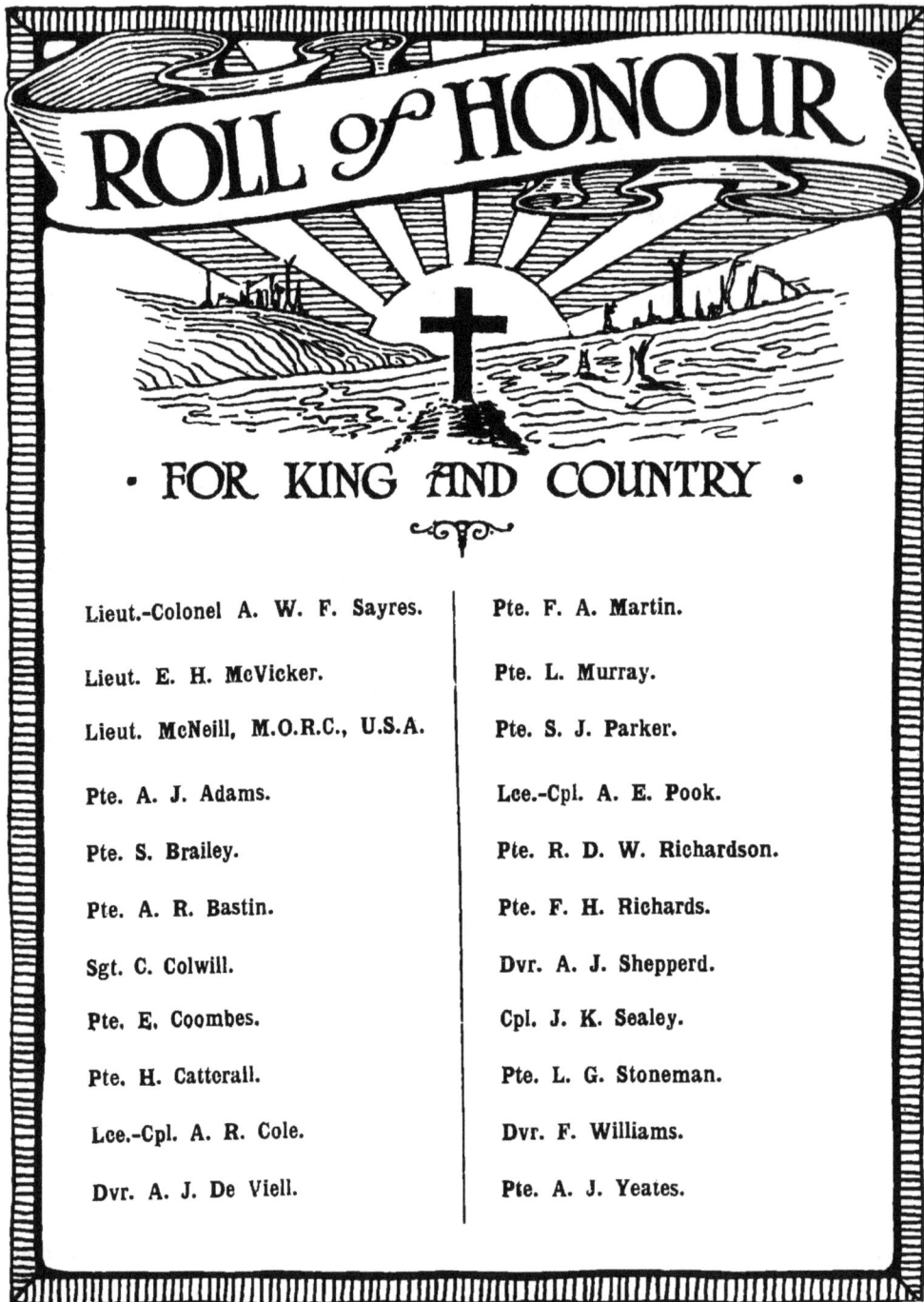

ROLL of HONOUR

· FOR KING AND COUNTRY ·

Lieut.-Colonel A. W. F. Sayres.	Pte. F. A. Martin.
Lieut. E. H. McVicker.	Pte. L. Murray.
Lieut. McNeill, M.O.R.C., U.S.A.	Pte. S. J. Parker.
Pte. A. J. Adams.	Lce.-Cpl. A. E. Pook.
Pte. S. Brailey.	Pte. R. D. W. Richardson.
Pte. A. R. Bastin.	Pte. F. H. Richards.
Sgt. C. Colwill.	Dvr. A. J. Shepperd.
Pte. E. Coombes.	Cpl. J. K. Sealey.
Pte. H. Catterall.	Pte. L. G. Stoneman.
Lce.-Cpl. A. R. Cole.	Dvr. F. Williams.
Dvr. A. J. De Viell.	Pte. A. J. Yeates.

Battle Casualties.

Owing to the state of flux into which the Unit was thrown by the process of rapid demobilization, it is quite possible that some names may have been omitted from the list hereunder, although the greatest care has been taken in compiling it.

WOUNDED.

Major Ellis, F. (twice)	Capt. Helby, E. H.	Capt. Smith, H. D. C.
Capt. Robinson, G. W.	Lieut. Staunton, G. P. W.	Lieut. Fismer, S.
Sergt. Essex, G. E. (3 times)	Pte. White, F.	Pte. Dicker, J. W.
Pte. Cawley, E. B. W. (3)	,, Woolcott, W. C.	,, McCully, W. A.
Sergt. Pearce, R. (2)	,, Kinrade, G.	,, Evans, S.
Staff-Sergt. Gee, W.	,, Clarke, J. H.	,, Bannerman, J.
Corpl. Bartlett, H. G.	,, Jackson, F. H.	,, Williams, J.
L.-Corpl. West, F.	,, Shattock, C. M.	,, Riley, J.
,, Jackson, R.	,, Baker, F. C.	,, Webb, W.
,, Bleby, C.	,, Cann, L.	,, Stocker, A. H.
,, Tolman, F. M.	,, Dymond, W. H.	,, Davies, G.
,, Harris, A.	,, Edworthy, R.	,, Aspey, P. W.
Pte. Glover, J. H.	,, Farmer, C.	,, Baker, W.
,, Bowers, F. L.	,, Hartley, F.	,, Clarke, W. J.
,, Beare, E.	,, Jackson, W. E.	,, Cann, E.
,, Extence, H. D.	,, Salter, S. C.	,, Harris, P. H.
,, Lang, C. V.	,, Madge, F. W.	,, Knapman, A.
,, Loosemore, A. E.	,, Thorne, H.	,, Pike, G. C.
,, Sanders, W. R. V.	,, Tucker, F. C.	,, Robinson, E.
,, Webb, B. T.	,, Cooper, W. R.	,, Pine, A. G.
,, Webber, W. J.	,, Jones, J.	,, Talbot, W. R.
,, Sampson, J.	,, Small, S. T.	,, Carr, J.
,, Williams, J. H. (accidentally wounded).		

R.A.S.C. ATTACHED.

Corpl. Trigg, W. A.	L.-Corpl. Taylor, A. H.	Dvr. Chown, S. F.
Dvr. Lawton, F. S. G.	Dvr. Daft, R. B.	,, Murton, G.
,, Pursey, N. C. S.	,, Bellis, J.	

PRISONERS OF WAR.

Pte. Jones, E. H.	Pte. Baxter, G.	Pte. Walker, A.
,, Lee, T. H.	,, Reynolds, R. S.	

A noteworthy point is that over 600 all ranks served in the Unit up to the Armistice, and when it is remembered that the full strength of a Field Ambulance is approximately 230, and we were usually under strength, it will be seen what a great wastage there was through death, wounds, disease and other causes.

Honours and Awards.

Bar to Distinguished Service Order.

Lieut.-Col. W. Blackwood, D.S.O.

Distinguished Service Order.

Lieut.-Col. W. Blackwood.

Bar to Military Cross.

Major F. Ellis, M.C.
Capt. J. A. Bell, M.C.

Military Cross.

Major F. Ellis.
Major E. Watson-Williams.
Capt. J. A. Bell.
Lieut. W. H. Jenks.

Distinguished Conduct Medal.

Sergt.-Major S. Bartlett.
Sergt. W. Pearce.
Sergt. C. R. R. Hancock.
Lce.-Corpl. F. Tolman.
Pte. E. Clemens.

Bar to Military Medal.

Sergt. G. E. Essex.

Military Medal.

Sergt. W. Pearce.	Pte. F. C. Fursman.
Sergt. R. Pearce.	Pte. W. L. Pidgeon.
Sergt. G. E. Essex.	Pte. A. H. Stocker.
Corpl. T. H. Matthews.	Pte. N. Morrell.
Corpl. H. G. Bartlett.	Pte. W. R. Stile.
Corpl. G. Hogan.	Pte. J. Sampson.
Corpl. W. A. Trigg.	Pte. W. H. Dymond.
Corpl. J. H. Lovesay.	Pte. R. E. Selway.
Lce.-Corpl. J. A. Slade.	Pte. G. Fraser.
Pte. W. R. Sanders.	Pte. P. E. Williams.

Meritorious Service Medal.

Sergt.-Major A. D. M. Savage.
Sergt. A. B. Trenear.
A/Corpl. R. Luxton.

Belgian Croix de Guerre.

Sergt. G. E. Essex.

French Croix de Guerre.

Sergt. A. B. Trenear.
Pte. J. McCullum.
Pte. C. Chapman.

Mentioned in Dispatches.

Lieut.-Col. W. Blackwood, D.S.O.
Major F. Ellis.
Major E. Watson-Williams.
Capt. J. A. Bell.
Capt. A. V. Stocks.
Sergt. F. H. Walters.
L/Sergt. H. Mitchell.

"A" SECTION.

November, 1918.

"B" SECTION.

November, 1918.

Wessex Comrades.

Although the war is over and we'll soon be leaving France,
We can't forget our comrades in the Wessex Ambulance;
We've "stuck it" well together in the years of stress and strife,
And our mem'ries will be vivid in the years of peaceful life.

We'll remember Colonel Blackwood and his fairly "cushy" ways;
He always had a cheery smile—a heartening word of praise.
He kept the Wessex "in the line," but when the work was done
He'd see they had amusements, and he joined them in the fun.

We'll remember Captain Strike and his famous "M. and V.,"
He wasn't such a bad old sort, with me you will agree.
Old soldier he, and with a short, sharp way with any "grousers,"
He got quite wild on Sundays, if you'd grease upon your trousers.

Then Major Watson-Williams, that terror on parade!—
If you only moved an eyelash, why, what a fuss he made!
If he hadn't been a doctor, he'd have made a soldier fine;
The boys all say he was a "trump" when working "up the line."

Then all the lads of Devon will remember "Daisy" Bell—
A pluckier there never was, he'd brave the mouth of Hell!
Of course, he had his funny ways, but no one is perfection,
And many a laugh he gave us at the Medical Inspection.

We'll remember Captain Robinson—a fav'rite with us all,
He took such interest in our sport, both hockey and football.
The happenings he'd seen in war would fill a massive tome,
He was first M.O. in Baghdad, and the first one in Salome.

We won't forget young Hinton, the amiable Yank—
He was a fine young officer without a trace of "swank";
And when he's sailed right back again across the silv'ry sea,
We know his Wessex memories among his best will be.

And then when we had trouble, and we needed counsel sage,
An ever sympathetic ear had Reverend Captain Page;
He always had a kindly word, be mornnig wet or fine,
With "Cheerio" he'd speed you as you set off "up the line."

When "Archie" got made S.M., didn't all the lads rejoice?
He had a lot of good points, but a most sepulchral voice!
"Jack" Woodman was his aide-de-camp; they formed a little league
For filling in the daylight hours by finding men fatigue.

Our "nom-coms" were good fellows, like all the men of Wessex;
At finding us new aid-posts, well, the best was Sergt. Essex;
His zeal in "forward areas" enhanced the Unit's fame,
And the bearers were stout-hearted and a credit to its name.

We won't forget the transport—Sam Bartlett's men so fine,
And our daring motor-drivers for their "clearing of the line."
They never shirked their duty, 'spite the strafing of the Boche,
They proved themselves to be always "sans peur et sans reproche."

In future years when present pals are scattered near and far
We won't forget the times we had together in the war;
We all had eccentricities, and now the flag is furled,
We realise it needed all to make our little world.

6th December, 1918.   D. McCALLUM, "A" Section.

History of the Unit.

CHAPTER I.

FORMATION AND TRAINING.

The 2/1st Wessex Field Ambulance was formed in September, 1914. At this time, the 1st Wessex Field Ambulance had been brought to War Establishment, and recruiting was proceeded with to form this Unit as a reserve. Both units were encamped on Perham Down, Salisbury Plain, and were inspected by His Majesty the King and the late Lord Kitchener at the latter end of September, 1914.

On October 11th the 1st Wessex Field Ambulance was posted to the 8th Division for Active Service. The 2/1st Wessex Field Ambulance then moved to Dawlish. Lieuts. F. Ellis, C. H. Maskew, J. A. Bell, C. J. E. Bennett and Lieut. and Transport Officer G. H. Tapper joined shortly after the Unit's arrival in South Devon. Lieut. and Quartermaster F. C. Strike was posted to it on November 8th, 1914. Major G. P. D. Hawker commanded until the 20th May, 1915, when he was succeeded by Captain R. Eager. Frequent drafts were provided for the 1st Wessex Field Ambulance, which by this time was the 24th Field Ambulance, B.E.F., having landed in France on November 5th, 1914. Recruiting proceeded at the Ambulance Headquarters at Holloway Street, Exeter. By the end of March, 1915, the War Establishment had been completed with the exception of the Officers. The men were raised principally from the County of Devon, Exeter, Teignmouth and Dawlish contributing largely.

A Bugle and Fife Band was started and trained by Staff-Sergt. Lamble, and this had a very successful career.

Prior to the departure from Dawlish to camp at Whitchurch Down, the Unit was inspected by Brigadier-General Lord St. Leven, Commanding the Wessex Division, who congratulated the Commanding Officer on its smart appearance. The Urban District Council and people of Dawlish at a public reception also expressed their high appreciation of the soldierly bearing of all ranks during their stay at Dawlish.

The Unit remained in camp at Whitchurch Down from the 20th May to the 6th October, 1915, the training at this Camp being much the same as at Dawlish, based on the R.A.M.C. "Manual." The Unit was inspected by D.M.S., Southern Command, and the G.O.C., Wessex Division. Lieut. Helby joined the Unit at this Camp in June, 1915.

The heavy rain during the latter part of the stay gave many a practical training for Active Service. Roads had to be constructed, and many footpaths made throughout the Camp. On October 6th the Unit moved to Teignmouth to go into billets.

The Headquarters at Teignmouth were provided at Bitton House, which offered good accommodation. A Brass Band was raised by Sergt. G. E. Essex, who acted as the Bandmaster, and martial airs resounded through the streets of Teignmouth at frequent intervals. The stay was short, but short as it was, the Unit became immensely popular with the Teignmothians, especially the fair sex, and it had a great send-off when we left for Larkhill on December 6th to equip for Active Service with the 55th Division.

At Larkhill, on the 11th January, 1916, the Command of the Unit devolved on Lieut.-Colonel A. W. F. Sayres, who came from the first-line Unit, where he had been second in command. The establishment of Officers was completed, and the Transport Officer, Lieut. G. H. Tapper, was withdrawn, while an additional Medical Officer was added.

After a month's stay the Unit entrained at Amesbury Station on January 14th, 1916, for Southampton and Active Service. The Channel was crossed during the following night.

F.C.S.

History of the Unit.

CHAPTER II.

INTRODUCTION TO ACTIVE SERVICE.

The Unit complete, with the exception that the seven Motor Ambulances had not been supplied before leaving the United Kingdom, landed at Le Havre on the morning of January 15th, 1916, after a very pleasant trip across the Channel. The disembarkation, with the long wait at the docks, and the trying march, with full kit, plus blankets, on the pavé through the town, up the steep and never-ending hill to the Rest Station, will always remain in the memory of the originals.

Early next morning the Unit was on the move to the Railway Station, to entrain for the Abbéville district, to join the 55th Division. The experiences of passing through places of historical and geographical interest on foreign soil, which for many was for the first time, and the special attention of "Young France" along the whole route, with the perpetual cry of "beeskwee—Anglaise," made this long, slow, and what otherwise would have been a tiresome journey in the "special" trucks provided, extremely interesting. The Unit reached Pont Remy at 8 p.m., after a twelve hours' journey in the "Express."

The Chateau at Liercourt was obtained for Headquarters and Hospital. The Hospital was opened on the next day, and "C" Section Bearers, under Lieut. E. H. Helby, were detached to run the Division Baths and Laundry at Bettencourt. Seven motor ambulances, in charge of Sergt. Morgan, joined the Unit. All the drivers had seen Active Service, attached to the 84th Field Ambulance of the 27th Division during the second Battle of Ypres, and they exhibited bullet-holes and shrapnel marks on their cars with pride.

The Division, being completed, moved to take over a portion of the Front Line from the French on the extreme right of the Arras Salient. The Unit left Liercourt on February 5th, followed the Somme to Longpré, passed over the river here to Domart, and arrived at Feinvillers after a twenty-mile march. The Hospital was opened here for a few days. On the 9th February, Sarton was reached through Hem and Doullens. With a night's rest at Humbercourt, the Unit, by a short march, reached Saulty, where the Hospital was established for a short time. •

The Division was now relieving the French in the Forward Area, and the Unit had the honour to be the first Field Ambulance of the three in the Division to have charge of the Forward Evacuation of sick and wounded. Captain F. Ellis, in charge of C Section, opened an Advanced Dressing Station at Bellacourt on the 13th of February. Collecting Posts were established at Wailly, The Brasserie, Le Fermont and Riviere. The Headquarters moved to Courturelle and opened the Divisional Main Dressing Station in the Chateau on the 16th February.

This was the Unit's first experience of Active Service, and although this particular Front was considered a quiet one, incidents occurred when the experiences of the Officer Commanding, with that of the motor ambulance drivers, proved invaluable. The Unit now found itself doing the work for which it had trained so long. It was fresh from "Blighty," full of enthusiasm, eager to be at work. It was not as yet suffering from that war-worn spirit which asserts itself after long continuous active service. "Nothing was so great, or difficult, but that it could be accomplished" was the motto of every one in the Unit.

The evacuation of wounded from the trenches was so prompt, day or night, that the "Wessex" Field Ambulance soon became well known throughout the Division. A foundation was being laid to the great reputation which the Unit has obtained for "Working the Line." By good fortune we suffered only one casualty while on this Front. Pte. W. R. Talbot received a nasty wound in the thigh by a fragment of a shell on the 18th of March, when the A.D.S. was being shelled.

Dressing Stations for Batteries, and Infantry Battalions on rest, were opened at Basseau and Beaumetz. It was at the last named place that Capt. E. H. Helby invented the "Helby" Dressing Box from tea and biscuit tins. This improvised box soon became well known throughout the British Armies.

One of the surprises of the Unit was to find that the civilians lived so near the "Firing Line." Bellacourt, a thousand yards from it, was inhabited. Wailly was the only place that came up to expectations. This village was nothing but a mass of ruins, being under direct observation from the enemy, who held the crest of the hill a thousand yards away. The sound of machine gun bullets on the ruins of the Church, as well as the sound of them

"WHAT DID YOU DO IN THE GREAT WAR DADDY?"
"AH, MY BOY — THAT'S WHAT EVEN YOUR MOTHER DOESN'T KNOW"

as they whistled overhead at "Suicide Lane," caused these places to be treated with respect. From experience since gained, it has been proved that ignorance made several brave in their actions while round Wailly.

One of the saddest cases of the many dealt with on this front was that of an old lady who was over seventy years of age. The enemy was strafing the next village, and bearers were summoned from the A.D.S. to collect a wounded case from this place. The impressions of the bearers as they entered the house for a wounded "Tommy," as they thought, only to find a grey-headed old lady lying on a stretcher, with extensive wounds on the right side, from head to feet, the right arm being gone, and her partner in life bending over her, can hardly be described. They will be stored with others in the memory, and will re-appear at times to portray the "Horrors of War" in its reality.

The Divisional Baths and Laundry were still run by detachments from the Unit. The Laundry was situated at Humbercourt, about three kilometres from Headquarters. Lieut. McVickers was in charge of this party, and those who worked under him will have many happy recollections of the work at Humbercourt, in spite of the many extra fatigues endured. The Bath staff at Gouy spent a jolly time. The monotony of bathing and supplying clean underclothing to a thousand men a day was relieved by rumours of leave to Blighty, as they were on the Divisional Headquarters leave allotment, which naturally had great advantages over that of the Unit in such matters. It is regretted that not one of the staff had a realisation of this dream for some months.

This detached work was never very popular with anyone. It caused one of the party to sketch the caricature on the previous page.

The Unit was relieved from the Forward Area by the 1/3rd West Lancs. Field Ambulance. For the few days rest, the Quartermaster commandeered the "spare" personnel at Headquarters to check and clean the Unit's equipment. This rest did not last long, for on May 6th, after a long route march, everyone was busy at Fosseau taking over the Corps Officers' and Divisional Rest Stations. These were situated in the Chateau, extra accommodation for the sick and slightly wounded being provided by large French huts built in the grounds. This proved to be the first and last time that such work in back areas fell to the lot of the Unit, its normal position being in the Forward Area. After settling to the work and time being obtained to enjoy the splendid walks through the magnificent woods and neighbourhood, to say nothing of the pleasure one derived from a shave by the lady barber of the village, the Rest Stations had to be moved, after less than a month's stay.

The Officers' Rest Station was transferred to the pretty little village of Manning. It has always remained a query why the work at this Hospital was so popular with all ranks, especially with the cooks. The Divisional Rest Station moved to Barley, where a Rest Station had been partly built. A lot of spade work was needed here to complete this Hospital and to bring it to the Wessex standard. After the whole-hearted support of all ranks this was soon accomplished, so much so, that when the Corps Commander paid a surprise visit to inspect, he complimented the Officer Commanding on the excellent work the Unit had done.

A.N.O.N.

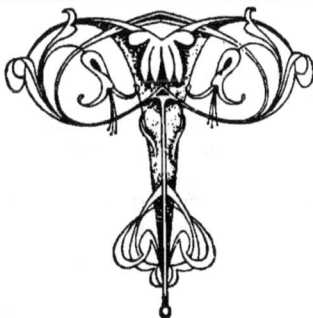

History of the Unit.

CHAPTER III.

THE SOMME, JULY, 1916.

Leaving Arras after a happy six months, we proceeded to what proved to be real war. No one who went from Arras to the Somme can ever deny the truth of that old saying "Ignorance is bliss." We had had our baptism of fire at Arras 'tis true, but "war" was as yet an almost unknown quantity in our lives, which is to say that we had yet to realise fully that our lives were an unknown quantity in war.

At Candas, after two days on the road, a considerate Commander gave us a lift in one of those trains so aptly described as "the trains with square wheels." Jolting and complaining, we rumbled over the flat, hedgeless scenery, sometimes looking out of the doors, and sometimes playing cards. At dinner-time, too, that eternal puzzle—the opening of a tin of "bully" with the opener sometimes provided—gave us a much wanted change from the monotony of the trip.

We came to many full-stops, but eventually we came to a fuller one, and after an hour's complaining at the long halt, were bustled into life by being ordered to "get your packs on." A short march then brought us to Treux, tents and a night's rest. Most of us managed to get a dip in the river next day, and the day after found us on our way to Méaulte, near which, on a bleak common, we spent a happy week listening to the dull thunder of the guns.

We then marched, by a very devious route, to West Péronne, seeing the ruins of Mametz and Fricourt on the way. Within a day or two we shifted slightly forward into a trench, and it was here that we had our first fatal casualty. Alfred Adams, a miner, was buried by a section of the bank of the trench, which gave owing to the concussion of the neighbouring big guns.

The panorama opened up to one on looking eastwards over the valley towards Guillemont Ridge was one of extreme grandeur. The picture—in various shades of grey—disclosed the Woods of Delville, Trones and Bernafay—mere groups of stumps and fallen branches. The roads, just discernible, seemed mere ribands lying on the ground. One followed with an intense interest the course of a galloping shell-limber, racing on its way over the shell-swept routes, while watching with concern the great, black "crumps" bursting at the crossings, and then when the limber emerged from the smoke still galloping on, one could have cheered aloud.

Here, too, we had our first "gas-alarm" one evening at dusk. We had had orders to "stand to" on the top of a parapet, and had the whole plain in front of us, jet black under the cloak of night, broken only by the dazzling flashes of the guns and the flickering radiance of the star-shells, making a picture that will remain imprinted on the retina of many an eye.

The Guillemont "stunt", so far as it affected us, recalls the memories of Happy Valley, Casement Trench, Dublin Trench, Death's Valley, and Chalk Trench.

Of Happy Valley we saw little enough; packed with big guns, it held little happiness for any; albeit, it was passed on our way to rest.

Going up to Casement Trench for the first time, I remember we were mainly interested in counting the dead horses by the roadside. Of Casement Trench itself the salient features were the stench, the crowd, the art of sleeping in a circle like a dog, and that "soft spot near the entrance."

Death's Valley we know only too well. Those three relay posts, those endless stretcher cases, the stunning shock of the guns, and the awful ominous shriek of coming shells will always remain with us.

"C" SECTION.

November, 1918.

OFFICERS, W.O.'s and SERGEANTS.

GRAS PAYELLE, AUGUST, 1917.

Capt. F. Ellis with "C" Tent Sub-Division were running the 5th Army Rest Station
at this time; hence some are absent from above photo.

Leaving the road, one bore to the right along a greasy track lined by tangled wire, pock-marked by newly-made shell holes. Clusters of dead caught one's eye and made one wonder at the folly of all war. Walking calmly up a valley strewn with dead, one felt overshadowed with impending doom, and war seemed stupendous folly. Still one walked on.

This valley, however, did not often invite contemplation. Times were when bursts of smoke alone were visible, when men, what men were there, lay flattened to Mother Earth wishing they had the cover of a trench. Flying shells do not speak so much of foolishness as of danger.

Then it had its funny side, had this Valley of Death—the breakfast burning in the pan for lack of fat, the petrol in the tea, and the needless ducking of some day dreamer startled into life by one of our own guns firing.

Comedy gave way to tragedy just before our relief arrived, for even while we were congratulating ourselves on our luck, the Dublin Trench affair occurred. Three good men of ours—Bert Yeates, Sam Parker and "Knebby" Coombes—were buried with a number of bearers from other Ambulances in the debris.

They died young, not facing fearful odds, but doing, unnoticed, that incomparable work which has earned for the Red Cross Man the esteem of the world.

A TRENCH AID POST.

One M.O. killed, one wounded, our three men and six more of the staff killed, it devolved on five of us, under the command of Sergt. W. Pearce, to carry on, the latter being awarded the D.C.M.

In the "Messages from Mars," the Rev. T. L. B. Westerdale describes his visit to Death Valley as follows :—

"Creeping along to the top of the ridge I came to what had been an ammunition dump, but with uncanny precision the Boches had put a fire-shell right on the dump, exploding thousands of rounds with terrific force and noise. I saw the fire-shell fall and do its terrible work only too well. Close to the dump were two human forms lying on their backs, faces upward to the sun. One was a lad not twenty years of age. . . . . He wore on his arm the familiar sign of the R.A.M.C. Next to him was an older man lying peacefully in the dust, the black smoke from the burnt out dump near him ascending in a straight column-like incense into the blue sky. On the arm of this man's tunic were the familiar letters 'S.B.' A regimental stretcher-bearer and a R.A.M.C. bearer had fallen side by side in the noblest of actions, on the very field of battle. . . . .

"Oh, the immortal glory of the stretcher-bearing men in the war ! Silence into shame with fiery words of rebuke the man who jests about the regimental or R.A.M.C. stretcher-bearer! Here on the very field of battle, I have seen them out and above the trenches hour after hour, by day and by night, fully exposed to thousands of shells and bullets, walking calmly along the pathways of hell, away down to the dressing stations. . . . .

"Here I have seen them fall and die, while others have calmly taken their places and carried their bleeding burdens on to safety."

The "Advanced" Dressing Station in Dublin Trench the above mentioned writer describes as follows :—

"The R.A.M.C. dressing-stations down the valley are full and busy now. As usual, these stations are in the midst of guns. It cannot be helped, but sometimes it increases the horrors of war. Shells bursting among the helpless wounded is the ghastliest of all sights. The wounded are coming in now from that part of the field close to the enemy's lines. The bearers are out in crowds searching every inch of ground. . . . . A road winding through this valley was the only highway for the infantry to one part of the line, and this road was lined with dead. We stumbled over the bodies in the darkness. Then we buried them, but stumbled over more the following night. . . . . . .

"On this road was the dressing station so dangerously situated among the guns. It seemed to us a miracle that it stood. Not one shell now and then, but one hundred an hour, fell within twenty yards of its sand-bagged entrance. An hour or two after I left the end came. The poor old shanty got a direct hit from a great crumper, and was a mass of smoking debris."

We entrained for rest at Maricourt, and after a whole day's travelling were turned out at some unknown station and commenced a never-to-be-forgotten march.

Starting with a hill, bad omen of worse to come, we covered some distance; but our village never seemed to come, although village lights appeared in the distance, drew alongside and passed behind with amazing monotony; and we began to feel the strain of past events. Packs nearly breaking our backs, wobbling at the knees, and with our feet tingling and sore, it is not to be wondered at that we lost our pride of march, some falling out by the wayside and spending the night in barn or ditch, awaiting daylight.

After what seemed an eternity of time, we who had persevered arrived at Fressenville. Fourteen days of "bearing," the march from the line, one night's rest, the train journey, and fifteen kilometres with full pack all made a creditable bit of work.

It was worth it, all the same. Green trees, houses, roads, neither a mass of holes nor lined with transport; girls and women with their refining influence, all spoke to us of peace and youth and happiness. Straight from the living hell of war we had stepped, under cover of the night, into a beautiful little French town and a welcome worthy of the times.

A new feeling of comradeship arose amongst us, each feeling how good it was to be alive, and a brotherly unity was formed from the common thankfulness and praise in our hearts.

At sunset, when we gathered and sang those part-songs, the heritage of every Briton, we were singing hymns of praise. We knew not why, neither did we care; but our happiness during that week was somehow sacred.

However, our rest, beautiful beyond words with the reaction of peace from war, was short and sweet; for we were soon to be put to the test again, but a merciful Providence saw that our happiness was marred by no foreknowledge.

Swift, unheralded by rumour, came the order—and on Sunday, seven days after our arrival, we were trekking it back again.

Entraining at Pont Rémy, of old and happy memory, we finally settled down at Bellevue Farm, on the outskirts of Albert, to recuperate from the fatigue of travel.

In this, our second "stunt," we used a "quarry" at the foot of Montauban, and formerly a German headquarters, as our A.D.S., working from it the evacuation of wounded from Delville, Trones and Bernafay Woods, and Green Dump. We also made an abortive attempt to dig a dug-out in a chalk cliff.

Amongst our multitudinous impressions, it is possible to say that Green Dump presented horrible difficulties in the form of mud, and that Bernafay Wood, a nest of batteries, was subjected to violent and sustained tear-shell bombardments.

But Delville Wood, then only partly in our hands, held the most dreaded post of all. Its bombardment ceased neither day or night. Life would have been impossible were it not for dug-outs, a few of which still remained. Even so the concussion of the shells continually put our candles out. One's sense of direction, too, was easily lost. Enemy trenches, levelled by the shell-fire, fallen trees and stumps, made landmarks difficult of selection.

On one occasion two squads of men were out seven hours fetching in two stretcher cases. Nearly lost, crawling on their stomachs around fallen trees, under machine-gun and snipers' fire, they eventually got back in another brigade's area—but with their wounded. Lce.-Corpl. Tolman, who was wounded and forced to crawl back alone before reaching the cases, was awarded the D.C.M.

At the same time Lieut. McVicker, a Canadian Officer much liked by all, was killed in Trones Wood.

Delville Wood, now named with the many other historical sites of superlative bravery in the field, was a veritable graveyard of both British and German. Supreme devotion to a cause never asked more of any man than the entering of such a death-trap. In retrospect even, humour has no place in connection with such an altar of sacrifice.

DELVILLE WOOD.

After a few days rest in the neighbouring back-areas we began the last and longest of our three " affairs."

Going forward over the old ground, we found that between Bernafay and Delville Woods, where once all had been destruction and desolation, a canvas town had sprung up. Where we had never dared to strike a match after the sun had set, could now be seen a myriad lights as though the very valley had been decked to celebrate the occasion with a fete. Horse lines and tractor parks occupied the places where machine guns and out-posts had been.

But as we passed on through Delville Wood and the ruins of Longueval, down into the next Valley, all was harsh and stern again. It was here, along this valley, that our " carry " lay. At once the longest, dirtiest and most dangerous we had ever experienced, it seems to challenge description.

Starting from what is even now referred to as the " 9th King's Aid Post," we proceeded across a field of shell holes to Scottish Trench, then along the Flers-Longueval road to the Funk-holes, and up the hill to Delville Wood and the waggons. On the Flers road we had to pass an 18-pounder gun on the crest of the road, and at the Funk-holes was a stranded tank, only we knew not what to call it until days after when we read about such wonders in the papers.

For a fortnight we worked night and day, dead tired, wide-eyed with sleeplessness, weary of mind, body and limb, presenting a sight less human every day, washing and shaving being impossible owing to lack of water.

We were strained nigh to breaking point when a hundred Liverpool Scottish, all volunteers, came to relieve us.

Twenty-four hours of deepest slumber followed, and then, still stiff and wet, we had perforce to start again.

After severe stunts, such as these were, we stretcher-bearers rarely finished our work until several hours after the division had gone out of action, and this proved to be no exception to the rule. We have the reputation for leaving no wounded behind for the relieving division to clear, and this time it was some two days later that we received word that we had finished, and could make off back behind the battle zone.

Turning our backs on the nightmare scene, we hurried to places of greater safety, and arrived tired and exhausted at Maricourt.

Our first business was to shave and wash, and we lay down to sleep feeling years younger after getting rid of a fortnight's growth of beard.

It was well that we shaved when we did, for early next morning we entrained en route for Ypres.

We came away with the feeling of the Village Blacksmith—that " something attempted, something done," had earned us our repose—at least such repose as Ypres had in store for us.

H. STOCKER.

POEM.

The Lord Who made the earth, the sea and sky,
Did once descend and leave those Thrones on high,
To be born of a Maid, and in a Manger lie,
Just to teach the sons of men to try
And live a life of good, and how to die.

Men heard a voice so sweet and calm and low,
On countless souls a comfort He'd bestow,
On those who serve and toil or reap and sow.
He gave the Word of Life to those in woe,
Which made them happy just to bear it so.

To-day while every nation wages war,
Grim death and terror reap abundant store,
And pluck the loved ones of both rich and poor,
Yet, speaks the Voice. They learn to love Him more,
To crave forgiveness, rest, when this life's o'er.

A. R. COLE.

(Somme, September, 1916).

Christmas, 1916.

AT HEADQUARTERS.

Christmas, 1916, will live long in the memory of everyone who was then serving in the Unit. We were placed in very fortunate circumstances, having ample facilities for amusements at Poperinghe, the hub of the Ypres sector. The following is quoted from a report which appeared in a Devonshire paper :—

AN ENJOYABLE TIME.

"It is a general opinion that a Christmas spent on active service, and under war conditions, lacks the spirit of merriment which attends the celebrations in Blighty, but if the opinion of men of the 2/1st Wessex Field Ambulance is accepted, then that idea will be quickly dispelled. For some time previous to Christmas, active preparations were made by our Committee, and the amount of enthusiasm displayed was in itself sufficient assurance of a fitting celebration of the most popular of all festivals.

On Christmas Day the sergeants waited on the men at the dinner table, and the men did full justice to sumptuous fare, a great deal of which was provided by the generous subscribers to the Mayoress of Exeter's Fund, and the 'Daily Telegraph' and 'Daily News' Funds. The menu consisted of roast beef, roast mutton, baked potatoes, cabbage, carrots, apricots and cherries, plum pudding and sauce, celery and cheese, followed by dessert. Following the example of the first line unit—the 24th Field Ambulance—a concert was arranged to crown the festivities. It was the first Christmas spent on active service by the Wessex boys, and no doubt fond parents at home readily imagined them having a very dull and indifferent time. But if they could have taken a glimpse at their 'boys' on Christmas evening they would have been quickly disillusioned. A Devonshire lad finds it natural to accommodate himself to circumstances, and wherever he is a spirit of liveliness never fails to assert itself.

"Under the expert (more or less) criticism of the sergeants of the unit (who left no effort unspared to make the affair an unqualified success), the artistes rehearsed their various parts to perfection, and the unstinted, whole-hearted applause accorded every item by the tightly-packed audience fully justified any further event of a similar nature they may promote.

"From first to last laughter was rippling through the building, and every item was greeted with well-merited appreciation and insistent demands for encores. The star turn was Pte. F. Tucker (St. Austell), who convincingly masqueraded as one of the fair sex. The amorous inclinations of those who were not 'in the know' were very persistent; indeed, a stranger, a Lancashire Tommy, actually craved an introduction. The 'feminine' impression was materially strengthened by the kindness of a lady who generously loaned the costumes. Sergt. Jos. Allen was 'Miss' Tucker's companion (viz., Sexton Blake, 'the great disinfector'), and his clever witticisms provoked roars of laughter. Another 'lady' was Pte. H. G. Shattock (Cullompton), who appeared in a screamingly funny sketch with Ptes. P. Ireland and C. Cobley (Exeter). Pte. Ireland, in the role of a medical officer conducting sick parade, exhibited histrionic ability of a high standard. 'Pat's' irresistible humour exuded at every pore, and his funny antics vied with the evolutions of the renowned 'Charlie.' His efforts as an amateur are well known to Exonians, and his period of active service seems to have added to his sense of humour. Corpl. Swimbourne, a versatile artiste of exceptional ability, contributed a couple of items, and won well-merited encores. His impersonation of Mr. Bransby Williams in ' Devil-may-care ' was particularly fine. Sergt. Frank Walter (Bideford) possesses an exceptionally sweet, well-balanced tenor voice, and was at the top of his form in ' Glorious Devon.' He gave as an encore ' I'll sing thee songs of Araby.'

" Sergt. Alf. Davey and Pte. J. Gibbings are both well-known to Dawlish audiences, and they respectively gave very pleasing renderings of ' The end of a perfect day ' and ' Blue Eyes.' Repetition does not detract in the least from the beauty of ' Comrades in Arms,' and the faithful interpretation given to it by the Wessex Glee Party—under the baton of Sergt. F. Walter, and accompanied at the piano by Sergt. R. S. Pearce—would do credit to a trained male choir. Sergt. J. Hard (South Brent) was at his best in ' Widecombe Fair,' and Staff-Sergt. Tustian (133rd Field Ambulance) delighted the audience with his comic song, ' Follow the tram lines,' and earned a well deserved encore.

" During an interval, the C.O. (Lieut.-Colonel A. W. F. Sayres), in the course of a neat little speech, wished the men the season's compliments, and paid a tribute to the energetic work of all who had contributed to their day's enjoyment. He especially eulogised the conscientious work of Lieut. and Qrmr. F. C. Strike, who devoted all his abilities to the welfare of the unit—(cheers). He (the speaker) had spent three Christmasses on active service, and each successive one had proved more enjoyable than its predecessor. But this, he hoped, would be the last—(hear, hear).

" Appended is the full programme : Pianoforte selections (popular airs), Lce.-Corpl. E. W. Cawley ; song, Pte. J. Gibbings ; comic song, Pte. G. Hooper ; song and step dance, Pte. Ryder ; farce, Ptes. Ireland, C. Cobley, and H. Shattock ; dialect song, Sergt. J. Hard ; impersonations, Corpl. Swimbourne ; comic song, Staff-Sergt. Tustian ; song, Sergt. A. J. Davey ; song, Sergt. F. H. Walter ; burlesque, Sergt. J. Allen and Pte. F. Tucker ; monologue, Sergt. J. Allen ; humorous sketch, ' Sick Parade,' Pte. P. Ireland (medical officer), Pte. C. Cobley (sergeant on duty), Lce.-Corpl. L. Cole (orderly), Lce.-Corpl. E. Cawley, Lce.-Corpl. J. Slade, Ptes. H. Ballan, W. E. Jackson and G. Hooper (patients), and Pte. Tucker (Mdlle. Peroxide) ; Glee, 2-1st Wessex Glee Singers, viz., Sergt.-Major L. J. Bartlett (Teignmouth), Staff-Sergts. L. Marks and S. Bastin (Exeter), Sergts. Davey (Dawlish), F. H. Salter (Exeter), J. Hard (South Brent), F. H. Walter (Bideford), A. Taylor (Teignmouth), Doidge (Brixham), Corpl. J. Tucker (Exeter), Lce.-Corpl. E. H. Cawley (Exmouth), Ptes. Ballan (Exeter), Kirk (Tiverton), Gibbings (Dawlish), F. Crispin (South Brent), and Ireland (Exeter) ; Sergt. R. S. Pearce accompanied. The pianist for the evening was Lce.-Corpl. E. W. Cawley. The proceedings terminated with the singing of the National Anthem."

H.E.G.S.

AT THE A.D.S.

On Christmas Eve everyone in the cellars of the ruins of the well-known Asylum at Ypres was eagerly looking for the arrival of rations (which usually came up by the evening relief Motor Ambulance Car) to see what Christmas fare would be provided. Rumours had been rife of the various things which were to mature, and the Ration Car was met by a willing and eager band of workers, all anxious to unload the stores.

Having unloaded, the party proceeded to split them up to supply the four R.A.P.'s and the A.D.S., it being soon found that, although the variety was good, the quantity was not. However, the R.A.P.'s were first served.

This done, the faces of those at the A.D.S. were far from wearing the Christmas look ! A brilliant idea of one of the lads, on Christmas morning, was soon put into execution. A Committee was formed of N.C.O.'s and men to collect subscriptions and arrange for purchases at the local Canteen, which was then well stocked. The N.C.O. in charge of the party approached the M.O., obtained permission to purchase, and incidentally relieved him of 10 francs towards the expenses.

A " scrounging " party was formed and was sent out. They provided vegetables, holly and evergreens from what had once been the lovely garden of the Asylum.

Members of the Committee proceeded to the Canteen and bought Christmas puddings, biscuits, fruit, cigars, cigarettes, etc. Meanwhile those remaining set to with gusto, and tastefully decorated the interior of our quarters.

Pte. L. Hore volunteered to fetch cakes for tea from the neighbouring village, and did remarkably well on this commission.

All turned to with a will on this Christmas morning, and the necessary work was soon done. Our cook (Pte. W. Hoare) had no lack of assistants, and served up a good old Christmas dinner, to which full justice was done. The menu of the dinner, compiled by the humorist of the party, was as follows :—

MENU.

1. Roast Beef. Bouef.
2. Vegetables. Pommes de Terres. Boiled. Roast.
Turnips.
Cabbage.
3. Entree. Fritz's Iron Rations.
4. Sweets. '' If it '' Pudding (Plum Duff).
5. Biscuits and Cheese.
6. Dessert. Oranges, Apples, Nuts, etc.
7. Cigarettes.
'' God Save the King.''

REVERSE.

Choice selection of Liqueurs.
Beer ! Beer !! Beer !!! Glorious Beer !
Tea, Cough'ee, etc., Vin du Naturale.

DONT'S.
Don't forget to bring your mess-tin.
— eat too much.
— be downhearted.

At dinner Capt. Crawford paid us a visit, and the usual toast and compliments of the season were paid ; while goodwill and jollity reigned, at least, on our side of the line. Fritz was very good, with just one strafe in the afternoon. We had only one casualty through on Christmas Day, the patient having a lovely Christmas-box (a '' Blighty ''), a bullet wound in the fleshy part of the forearm.

The afternoon was spent in the usual English style. A most laughable competition was indulged in at tea-time between Ptes. Kellow and Beavis. Those who were there will remember this, and many a hearty laugh will they have over it.

The evening was passed with a sing-song, in which everyone tried to do his bit. Cards and other games were also indulged in.

The remarkable feeling of goodwill and comradeship between all ranks on this occasion proved that our experiences on the Somme had not made us war weary, or stultified our capacity for enjoyment, though of a primitive order, owing to locality and surroundings in general.

Thus we spent our first and last Christmas actually in the Line.

G. E. ESSEX.

History of the Unit.

CHAPTER IV.

YPRES.

What visions the word "Ypres" conjures up before our eyes! What memories it revives!—The Unit left the Somme on the 29th September, 1916. Entraining at Ribemont, we passed Corbie (where a few of our men were attached to a Casualty Clearing Station for a few days), and the lovely city of Amiens, detrained at Longpre, and marched to Epagne, where we stayed a couple of days, and where the Unit lost the services of the Motor Transport, which had been attached since our arrival overseas.

On the 2nd October, 1916, we entrained at Abbeville, en route for Ypres, and detrained at Proven on the 3rd October. The same evening "B" Section left for the first tour of duty in the famous Ypres Salient. The A.D.S. at the well-known Asylum, with the R.A.P.'s and R.P.'s at Menin Road, West Lane, Poteyje, St. Jean and on the bank of the famous Yser Canal, were taken over.

The main body left the following day, marching to Poperinghe, and took charge of the M.D.S. at "The College" in the Rue de Boeschepe. Here we spent our first Christmas on active service, and our only one "In the Line" (accounts of which will appear elsewhere).

The Motor Transport from the 29th Division, in charge of Sergt. A. B. Trenear, were attached to the Unit for duty on our arrival here.

Things were quiet in those days, although there was always an uncertainty about this part of the line which one never felt elsewhere. Scarcely a day passed that Fritz did not pay some attention to the historical city, usually by sporadic outbursts, and occasionally by a short sustained bombardment. One always remembers the notices like

NOTICE!
DO NOT LOITER
HERE!
DANGEROUS!

posted in notorious danger spots, e.g., the SQUARE, in certain streets, at cross roads, and at the level crossing, in this ruined city of Ypres, any account of which would be unfinished did it not contain some reference to the famous Halles and the Cathedral with its one remaining tower, which stood so long in solitary grandeur, a monument of the city of the dead.

On 4th January, 1917, the Unit left for Herzeele for a rest (who will forget the bitter cold weather experienced there?) returning to the same position five weeks later. The stay lasted until the 16th April, during which time the area was becoming appreciably warmer, two shells falling in the M.D.S. at the College, one carrying away the Officers' Latrine. The enemy now began to shell Poperinghe at frequent intervals, but fortunately the Unit did not suffer any casualties.

While we were in this Salient a small detachment from the Unit ran the Divisional Baths and Laundry in Poperinghe, with a branch in Ypres itself. Lieut. E. H. Helby was the officer in charge until wounded in Poperinghe in July, which necessitated his evacuation to "Blighty."

On 16th April the Unit returned again to Herzeele, en route for Eperlecques with an Infantry Brigade, for special training in preparation for the coming battle, variously described as "Third Battle of Ypres," "Passchendaele Ridge," etc. Returning, it was found that the Divisional A.D.S. and M.D.S. were then situated at the Prison, Ypres, and Red Farm, on the Ypres Road near Vlamertinghe, which was very fortunate for the Unit, as about this time the cellars at the Asylum, the old A.D.S., and the College in Poperinghe, the old M.D.S., were both partially wrecked by enemy bombardment, causing several casualties to the medical units in occupation.

Horse Transport, R.A.S.C. (attached).

NOVEMBER, 1918.

Mechanical Transport.

NOVEMBER, 1918.

The salient now got warmer, the enemy trying by every possible means to harass our preparations for the coming battle. Aeroplane raids, bombing and reconnaissance, with attacks on observation balloons, and artillery bombardments all gradually increased in depth and intensity, till such a pitch was reached that one wondered how any living thing, either man or beast, could be left alive, and yet up to the eve of the battle civilians lived as near the line as Vlamertinghe.

The deeds of valour performed during these days were numerous. Many, like the desert flower, were " born to blush unseen," and will never be known. Daily, nightly, aye, many times daily, the cry of " stretcher bearers " rang through the Prison, and was as frequently and promptly answered.

Such was the conduct, noble and unselfish, of our lads, that it moved a Padre to write the following piece of poetry :—

A TRIBUTE TO THE R.A.M.C.

Out into the darkness of the night they go,
Fearless and bold.
They have heard the agony cry,
The call of a fallen comrade;
And out they go, into the night,
Into the dark night of Hell,
Into the hurricane of shot and shell,
To snatch from the very jaws of death
The fallen friend and comrade.

C. B. PIKE, C.F. (R.C.),
(The Prison, Ypres, May, 1917).

One must also give credit to the Motor Transport, both drivers and orderlies. Every day without fail they came to collect casualties, and brought up the rations, mails, and medical necessaries and comforts, no matter what the state of the roads, or how heavy the shelling. Too little is heard of these men, who with the bearers share the chief honours of the day. The Tent Sub-Divisions must not be forgotten, and they were, at this time, taking turns to staff the A.D.S. as well as the M.D.S.

The M.D.S., situated, as it was, on the Ypres Road, was not without its dangers and hardships. The enemy at times seemed to have tried to give exhibition shelling. How to place shells all round a Field Hospital without hitting it seemed to be the Huns' game. This was done several times, shells dropping only a few yards outside the hospital, so that the iron roofs of the huts with the falling stones, earth and iron early in the morning often sounded a premature reveille. The enemy's fire became so accurate that shells pitched in the " lines " on two or three occasions, fortunately without wounding anyone, the one which landed in the " Personnel Lines " proving a " dud."

During one of the enemy aerial visits a British anti-aircraft shell, failing to explode, fell in the Hospital and killed Pte. Martin, one who was much liked and greatly missed, and who had been with the Unit since the early days of its formation.

The M.D.S. had to be prepared for the great battle. A Gas Centre was established. The Surgical Ward was transformed to a Dressing Room and Evacuating Station. A Reception Room and Clerical Offices were also arranged, and everything at our Station was ready for what was, from the administrative point of view, probably the largest operation ever undertaken by the Unit single-handed, as this Divisional Main Dressing Station was on the eve of the battle made into a Corps' Main Dressing Station.

After the battering the old Prison received on the 28th June, it was considered advisable to move the A.D.S., and it was transferred to four dug-outs on the bank of the Yser Canal.

July 13th, 1917, was a very warm summer's day, and will be specially remembered for the enemy's gas attack. Mustard gas was used for the first time, and it must be confessed caused a good few casualties at this time. Gas casualties were never again collected in such numbers, this being chiefly owing to the men's confidence in the Box Respirator.

Medical preparations were being made forward, in front of the A.D.S., and it was when making these that the Officer Commanding, Lieut.-Colonel A. W. F. Sayres, received the wounds from which he eventually died in Hospital at Abbeville.

Everyone keenly felt the loss of the Colonel. Taking over command of the Unit only four days before embarkation for Active Service, he piloted us through the period of practical training on the Western Front. His previous experience with the 24th Field Ambulance on this same front proved invaluable, and gave everyone absolute confidence in him. It is to Lieut.-Colonel Sayres that the Unit owes the foundation of its great reputation for " Line work."

Lieut.-Colonel W. Blackwood was posted to the Unit as Officer Commanding. He came on active service with the 25th Field Ambulance (1/2 Wessex Field Ambulance) on November 5th, 1914, and for some time he had been O.C., 24th Field Ambulance.

The Unit was very fortunate in having such a successor to Lieut.-Colonel Sayres. We were " standing to " waiting for " Z " Day and Zero hour of a great engagement. The new Commanding Officer had just arrived, when orders were issued that the Divisional Main Dressing Station would be made a Corps' Main Dressing Station, and run by the unit. As Lieut.-Colonel Blackwood had obtained valuable experience as O.C. 24th Field Ambulance of Field Ambulance work in " Open Warfare," when the 8th Division followed up so smartly the retreating enemy on the Somme, in the spring, 1917, he was also placed in charge of the bearers' work forward. Great things were expected of this engagement.

Preparations to meet the new conditions were completed " Forward " and at the C.M.D.S. also. The A.D.S. was moved to the " Mine Shaft " at Wieltje. The difficulty experienced in getting up the stores via the light railway, and the large fatigue party necessitated by the line being blown up in several places, are some of the many incidents of the preparation.

The day of the opening of the battle, " Z " day, was the 31st July, and will be remembered by all who took part in it. Fine, dry, summer weather had prevailed before this, but " Z " day opened with a dull sky, and with that kind of rain well-known in Flanders (and the West Country !), guaranteed to last a month. Thenceforth the mud probably stood out most prominently even above the bombardment.

" Mud." The word hardly describes it ! Thigh deep, sloshy mud, with the general discomfort of torrents of rain, were the conditions under which the " Bearers " worked. Six and eight men were detailed to a stretcher, and then the pace would only be a crawl. Anyone who saw the Infantry or the Stretcher Bearers return from this action on August 4th, after working in these conditions for five days, would scarcely have recognised them as British soldiers. Uniforms could hardly be distinguished, so every Bearer was supplied with a new uniform and new underclothing from head to foot.

The wounded were in nearly as bad a condition on arrival at the C.M.D.S. Dry, clean stretchers and blankets were ready for the patients after they had been stripped, washed, their wounds dressed, and clothed in pyjamas. After some warm food had been given, the patient was sent on his way by car to the C.C.S., a new man.

Half-a-dozen of the men of the Unit received decorations for bravery during this engagement. Unfortunately, we lost three lads, in addition to having several wounded.

On August 4th the Unit moved to Watou, en route for Gras Payelle, entraining at Abeele, and detraining at Audrick. Gras Payelle was reached on the 6th August, and here we spent a pleasant month. The reaction after the stress was naturally great, but this was overcome by the programme arranged—Divisional and Unit competitions in football and various other sports, and last, but not least, those day trips to Calais. Even here, in the midst of the natural beauty of a lovely country hamlet, with harvest in full swing, trees and vegetation of all varieties in full bloom, we were not allowed to forget. Fritz came over the area with his large bombing planes. The only damage they succeeded in doing, however, was to knock out a few Chinese from the Chinese Labour Company near by.

As all good things end, so the time here ended all too quickly, in spite of the general inoculation with T.A.B. We returned once more to the Salient, an advance party leaving on September 14th (B Sec. Tent Sub.)—Who said rations ? Tut ! Tut ! !—The Unit followed the next day.

The Corps' Main Dressing Station was still at Red Farm, and the A.D.S. at Wieltje. The Bearers moved forward, while the Tent Sub-Division had the help of one Tent Sub-Division from each of the other three divisions of the Corps to help at the Corps' Main. Walking wounded were being treated at Vlamertinghe as in the previous stunt.

During our long stay (twelve months) in the Salient, Capt. C. J. E. Bennett acted as sanitary officer in charge of Ypres. Incinerator after incinerator was knocked out by enemy shell-fire. In fact, had the Hun endeavoured to keep a chart recording those destroyed, he would have had his work cut out !

This was probably our shortest stay in the line, for the Unit left again on the 26th. This time, it was to leave the Salient for good. After a day or two at a camp at Nine Elms, near Poperinghe, we left by train for the Somme Area once more. The Unit detrained at Bapaume, and marched to Barastre, where a stay was made for a few days. The Division now moved to its new front, midway between Cambrai and St. Quentin. Our Headquarters was in Villers Faucon, where we ran the Divisional Main Dressing Station. We also cleared the Forward Area from Epéhy and Lempire.

G.E.E.

Poperinghe Days.

Ypres—the very name has a sinister sound, recalling ruin, tragedy, the sweat and grime of war. "Wipers" will ever be associated with the heroism of the Contemptibles, the added lustre throwing into yet deeper relief the darker associations. Conjure with the word, pronounce it "Eeps," "Y-per," as you will, grim horror is woven into each syllable. How different with Poperinghe! Truncate it to "Pop," and you rob the name of its gloomy suggestions. To us it will always be "Pop." How reminiscent it is of jolly good times at the back of the front, the more enjoyable since they afforded some contrast to our experiences in the inferno of Ypres.

October, 1916, found us in Poperinghe. Our mettle had been tested in the red horror of the Somme. Yet another war winter loomed darkly ahead. The Salient had an evil reputation. For the moment the fires of hate were but smouldering. Who knew when they would blaze with redoubled fury? But we had learned to live in the present. The present was bright. The future could take care of itself.

What luck to be stationed in a big town! This place with its M.F.P.'s, its Town Guard, its theatres, its streets thronged with soldiers, had something of the air of an English garrison town, and small wonder! Since October, 1914, British division had relieved British division in the salient. The Belgians had grown accustomed to us, knew our wants, spoke our language. No need now of those clumsy French phrases, so hardly learned, so easily forgotten. "Biére speciale" now became "Special Beer." Alas! that otherwise it remained unchanged—"that which by courtesy we call beer." One could get a good dinner in Pop. Were your tastes epicurean you dined at "Skindles" or the "Hotel des Allies." Who has forgotten Antoinette's custard tarts, Marie's chips and eggs, done to a turn, or the roast pork and green peas of that restaurant in the Abeele Road?

We all remember those estaminets, their noisy, jostling crowds, their laughter and song; to say nothing of their bad beer! What tales could be told of them, in particular of one on the Proven Road. Who has forgotten those roystering Anzacs rolling a barrel of beer along by the College at midnight, shouting loudly for buckets and glasses? Alas! that after providing a bucket that beer should have been wasted.

There was a vast difference between the dull French villages and this gay town; between those draughty rat-ridden barns and the dormitories of the College! How comfortable we could have made those cubicles had we but known for how long we were to remain.

Oh! those stentorian shouts of the Guard as he woke us. If back in civil life our landlady would call "Rise and shine, my lucky lads!" how we should jump to it! Shall we ever forget how madly we rushed down those steep stairs when the Sergt.-Major's whistle sounded for parade, and heavy with sleep we scurried out into the chill, foggy courtyard? Then how we remember the musicians among us who were well content to be able to play the chapel organ, which was so soon to be reduced to a mass of torn, twisted pipes by a Boche 5.9!

The morning sick parades seemed daily a greater attraction. and occasioned no little profanity. Why did all the patients seem so dense—dental cases especially? Let me here set down the story of how a certain N.C.O., who shall be nameless, reproved their exceeding dullness. Three times he had called the roll of dental cases, adding the names of newcomers. Apparently everyone was accounted for. The party was just marching off when up came another man. "Did you call for dental cases?" he asked. "I've been waiting an hour." The N.C.O. thus addressed turned sharply on the luckless patient. "Oh! have you?" he replied. "I suppose you didn't hear me shout three times for dental cases. You stick there among the crowd of other patients and expect me to know—by some intuition—that you are a dental case. I'm not a thought reader!" Then, slowly and emphatically, he added, "What you fellows want is a ruddy sheep-dog to collect you —not an N.C.O.!"

Happy were those of us who, untroubled by dental cases, undismayed by the line of patients awaiting hot foments, worked at the Divisional Laundry! It must have been a delight to work with fair, slim Louise, to assist Gabrielle at the boiler, to live in the smile of Rachel. Who was the favoured fellow who won the esteem—nay, the love—of that plump damsel in a pink blouse? (I don't know her name. She lived near by Red Farm). They were so passionate, quick to love, quick to hate. Was it Spanish blood that made Marguerite so quick with a stiletto? Heavens! those brawny arms needed no knife; of themselves they could make one uncomfortable. And what of the laundry Christmas dinner and the dance that followed? Would the word "hobnail" describe it? Ah well! no longer does the post bring us picture-postcards bearing endearing messages. Marguerite, Louise, Julia have other gallants by now. We have been given our congé.

How we enjoyed Christmas at Pop! We kept it in true British style. The good roast beef of old England, the festive plum pudding, real beer with a head on it—none of your Flemish stuff— nuts and oranges, made a royal repast. Those who played football after that dinner were heroes. The evening's entertainment was excellent—"a direct hit." What lively recollections we have of the be-ribboned Sergeant-Major, the dashing Capt. Pat, the fascinating Mlle. Lizzie Dripping and the other actors in "Sick Parade." How badly we overrated the strength of the strong man! What a denouement on the shout of "The A.P.M.'s coming!" Truly it was a very merry Christmas.

But what would Poperinghe have been without "Talbot House"? The name recalls a flood of memories grave and gay. When life seemed dull and purposeless, when we were unutterably "fed up," Talbot House, with its opportunities for recreation, restored our spirits; and, by subtle suggestions which appealed to our highest instincts, aroused our flagging faith. There was something about the place that stamped it as being far removed, vastly different to a mere soldiers' club. Behind its every activity, behind every appeal was a personality, never obtrusive, but brimful of·magnetic force—Mr. Clayton. In his vocabulary the word "Tommy," with all its implications, had no place. Over the door of his study was the warning "All rank, abandon ye who enter here," a warning no one ignored; and divested of rank—whether high or low—we assumed the common dignity of man.

When in December, 1915, the Queen's Westminster Rifles built Talbot House Chapel they "builded better than they knew." Long months of parade services held in draughty barns or bare schoolrooms left us hungry for services in which dignity and beauty should attend devotion. Here we found both. Never will any war memorial, however conceived, however fashioned, be so filled with associations of our gallant dead, as was this spot, where, all sense of self subdued, we seemed possessed by an overmastering sense of their very presence. Among the chief of our impressions of Poperinghe, some vague, some clearly defined, some grave, some gay, many of us will ever preserve this final impression—solemn, inspiring, ineffaceable.

D. R. McM.

THE CLERKS' LAMENT.

There may be some who envy feel
  For those who drive the quill all day,
And wish they could their places steal:
  Just wait and listen to my lay.

We have no time to call our own,
  And must know all, and sometimes more,
From Orders after years have flown,
  To those still kept in future's store.

In times of "stunts" we've got to hustle
  From morn to night, without respite,
Or in the midst of all the bustle
  We'll get a wire: "Please expedite!"

It's just the same when on the "move,"
  No matter in what place we be;
A late return—that wire of love,
  "Please expedite B. 2, 1, 3."

When others have their well-earned "rest,"
  And precious time for sport and play,
The "powers that be" then do their best
  With New Returns the clerks to slay.

We thought the Armistice would prove
  A friend indeed, but bless your eyes,
Before an eyelid we could move
  The Order came: "Demobilize!"

The Army Forms came in a flood;
  We've got them all from A's to Z's,
And still they come, until we think
  They'll fairly drive us off our heads.

A kindly thought we humbly crave
  From all who read these simple words,
For those who found an early grave,
  Sent there by Army Forms—not swords.

A.B.M.

History of the Unit.

CHAPTER V.

THE OPERATIONS ABOUT CAMBRAI.

On November 20th, 1917, General Byng launched his attack on the German lines in front of Cambrai. The Division was not concerned in the general attack, the special features of which do not therefore call for remark here. Our task was to create a diversion further south, about midway between Cambrai and St. Quentin, so as to help to mask during the beginning of the attack the real objective. The 1/4th K.O.R.L.R. attacked Guillemont Farm, the 1/8th K.L.R. the Knoll, while the 1/10th K.L.R. (Scottish) attacked the line between the two.

The attack was made with a minimum of infantry and artillery on very strong positions; and although the enemy lines were entered, by evening our position was as at the start, in spite of reckless gallantry, resulting in heavy casualties. Capt. Watson-Williams, with 16 men of the ambulance, was in charge of evacuations on the right. Capt. Ellis was in charge of the A.D.S. at Lempire, and also of the sixteen men who cleared the left. The fighting died down during the afternoon and the evacuations produced no features of special interest.

In the early dawn of December 30th—a day memorable for the celebration all over England of a glorious victory—the Germans launched their double counter-attack at Cambrai, designed to cut the line north and south of the salient created by our main successful attack, and to " pinch off " the forces engaged in it. After a short bombardment, the line was pierced at Villers Guislain, and the enemy poured through in masses, overwhelming the small garrisons of the posts in support, and turning the left flank of the Division. In the first onset they captured Capt. Clements-Smith and several bearers of the 1/3rd W. Lancs. F. Ambulance.

About 8-30 a.m. rumours of disaster began to reach the M.D.S. Capt. Watson-Williams with Capt. Helby and 60 bearers from our own and the 2/1st W. Lancs. F. Amb. were ordered to St. Emilie to open an A.D.S.

The serious nature of the situation can be gauged from the secret orders given : (1) Not to advance from St. Emilie until it was certain that Epéhy remained in our hands ; (2) To be prepared to withdraw at once, jettisoning equipment if necessary ; (3) Officers to carry pistols.—The dressing-station was duly opened, and leaving Capt. Helby in charge, Capt. Watson-Williams arrived in Epéhy at 6 p.m. with 40 bearers.

What had happened that day? The 1/4th L.N. Lancs. had maintained a defensive flank on the north of the Division all day! The battalion in the evening consisted of two of the original companies, some details sent up from 164th Brigade transport, a platoon of the 1/10th K.L.R., a company of the 10th Buffs, and part of a company of the 4th Queens, the last two from the division on our left, which had been overrun.

During the night, all casualties were cleared by the exertions of the bearers—a prelude to three days very heavy work—and the cavalry sent to reinforce us arrived.

The next day found us in the same positions, but much better held. The 1st Canadian Cavalry Brigade and the Secunderabad Cavalry Brigade were dismounted, and held the trenches. The Lucknow and Umballah Brigades rode in magnificent fashion against the machine-guns of the enemy. One brigade got its attack home, and one was driven back by a rain of lead—but both suffered very heavy casualties, and in addition there were those of the infantry.

Peiziére, near Epéhy, was an appalling sight at noon. A cavalry brigade was in the village under heavy fire, and wounded and dying men and horses were lying everywhere. A cavalry A.D.S. —the only one established—was in the heart of the confusion, and was crowded with cases. It was cleared by the fine efforts of our M.T. drivers and one of the 1/3rd W. Lancs. drivers. All day long our bearers worked, usually in the open, and by midnight again, every available casualty was brought in. Sergt. Woodman was particularly concerned in the arranging of bearer parties all this time. Throughout the whole period Epéhy and the roads leading to it were being heavily shelled ; and the frenzied struggles of wounded horses constituted a not inconsiderable danger. During this period the Ambulance cleared several thousand casualties, most of them after the first day being from other formations than the 55th Division.

On December 2nd and 3rd the Division, which had consolidated its position, was taken into reserve, and a period of great stress and peril—and not a little anxiety—was at an end. We moved by road to the area around Bomy, where we were left in reserve to recuperate and refit. During the march, the transport covered in one day and without a meal 26 miles, parading at 6-30 a.m. and bivouacing in a very muddy field at 3-30 a.m. next day—a very memorable event, the trials of which were only partially mitigated by a very providential issue of rum in the "bivouac."

The Medical Personnel proceeded from Peronne by train to Montenescourt on December 8th. Berles was reached by road two days later, billets being secured for single nights at Brias on the 11th and Heuchin on the 12th. Audincthun was reached on the 13th of December.

The Unit established H.Q. and Brigade Hospital at the last-mentioned place. Here Football Leagues and Winter Sports of all kinds were in full swing. The unit football team proved to be the "runners-up" at the end of the Infantry Brigades' League competition.

The Unit remained at Audincthun until February 7th, 1918, thus having the pleasure of spending an "Xmas" on rest, with all personnel assembled at H.Q.

E.W.W.

THE CYNIC AND HIS CURE.

I fain would tell of a certain youth,
Born in a certain town,
The certain ideas of whom forsooth
Were as one of some great renown.

Now this strange lad was of humble birth ;
But the theme I have to tell,
A moment of your time is worth,
To hear what to him befell.

Of humble birth, but gentle, good,
Ingenuous and refined,
An obstacle in his pathway stood,
And that was his own mind.

How strange to one of such parentage
Whose instincts were the best,
That hungry longing would engage
To rob him of his rest.

A baron, esquire, or knight of shire,
Some lord of high degree
Were included in this strange desire,
A grand noble would he be.

September, 1916.

Alas ! one day the clarion note,
The cry of war goes forth,
For every man a soldier's coat,
A chance to prove his worth.

Shortly he takes his place in rank,
To learn to shoot and fight ;
Of strenuous life to the full he drank,
Nor was his burden light.

The life is hard ; the rule is stern ;
All comforts are debarred ;
His pride is hurt, he has to learn
A master to regard.

"Life's one long bore," he often sighs,
With that listless ennui ;
And curses all the martial ties
As boundless as the sea.

He faces death and darksome fear,
The terrors of the night,
And *now* he holds life all too dear,
He's found a second sight.

A. R. COLE.

Christmas, 1917.

Xmas this time came in good old-fashioned style, with plenty of snow and frost, and found the Unit in a small straggling French village named Audincthun, situated some miles to the rear of the La Bassee front. Small seemed the prospects of " Jolly good cheer.'' However, thanks chiefly to Col. W. Blackwood (who since the last Xmas had succeeded Col. A. W. F. Sayres) and the generosity of the civilians, who kindly lent various articles of apparel for the concert party, and placed the village schoolroom at the Unit's disposal for the dining and concert hall, this was not the case.

The Unit made very merry indeed, and obtained thorough enjoyment. The Officer Commanding organised and led a snow-fight. How he did enjoy it—as everyone did ! The dinner, thanks to the Quartermaster's Department, the Regimental Funds, and the noble efforts of the cooks, was a huge success, and voted by all as excellent. Col. W. Blackwood, in his speech, told us how proud he was to command the Unit, and how all ranks had helped to accomplish the strenuous tasks which the Unit experienced since he had taken command. We replied with cheers and sang " For he's a jolly good fellow " with a right hearty goodwill, as the O.C. was regarded as one to be proud of and a comrade to us all. Never a happier family ever gathered together than did the " Wessex " on this occasion.

It was at this Festive Season that the Concert Party attained its zenith of fame, and really surpassed itself. The programme provided was an exceptionally good one, and went with a swing from start to finish. It was as follows :—

PIANOFORTE SOLO		PTE. CAWLEY.
CONCERTED ITEM	" Jolly Good Luck "	
SONG	" Four and Nine " ...	... PTE. SMEATH.
SONG	" The Grey North Sea " ...	... PTE. J. GIBBINGS.
STEP DANCE		PTE. GOLDSWORTHY.
SONG	" My Word ! " ...	LCE.-CORPL. L. COLE.
SONG	" The Floral Dance " ...	... CORPL. VERITY.
SONG	" Come Back to Me " ...	PTE. H. PHILLIPS.
SKETCH	" The Crystal Gazer " ..	PTES. ILLINGSWORTH AND TUCKER.
SONG	" God send you back to me "	SERGT. A. J. DAVEY.
SONG	" The King's Own " ...	S.-SERGT. MARKS.
QUINTETTE	" Cottage by the Sea " ...	SERGT. TAYLOR'S PARTY.
SONG	" The Grenadiers " ...	... CORPL. VERITY.
SONG	" Down Texas Way " ...	... PTE. J. GLOVER.
DIALECT STORY	SERGT.-MAJOR S. BARTLETT and SERGT. J. HARD.	
SONG	" Dance with your Uncle Joe " ...	PTE. SMEATH.
SONG	" Devon " ...	SERGT. F. H. WALTERS.
FINAL SKETCH	" Leave it to me " ...	PTE. IRELAND'S PARTY.
	" GOD SAVE THE KING."	

It is very difficult to pick out the best of the items, but one or two may be specially mentioned. Pte. H. Phillips with " Come Back to Me " had a great ovation which required an encore. Pte. Glover's rendering of " Down Texas Way " quite took the audience by storm, and those U.S.A. medical officers attached to the Unit were greatly pleased with it. The two sketches proved very successful. " The Crystal Gazer " was a short sketch on fortune telling. Pte. Illingsworth made an excellent clairvoyant, while Pte. Tucker took the part of a charming lady with great effect.

Pte. Ireland and the " old gang " in " Leave it to me," a clever sketch on that much-abused theme " Love," its trials and difficulties, and the usual " happy ever after " ending, were in wonderful form and received quite the ovation of the evening. Lce.-Corpl. J. Slade, as Mr. Easy, the father of the heroine, performed the part with true effect. Pte. Shattock, as Amelia Easy, the heroine, was easily the nicest " girl " that the lads had seen for some time. The ardent lover—Pte. H. Rose—with his winning ways, had the entire sympathy of the audience. Pte. G. Hooper, as Mr. Quince, a blunt matter-of-fact old gent., was great.

Pte. T. Tucker and " Pat " Ireland, as Susan Muggins and Joe Sprouts respectively, kept the lads roaring with laughter with their course of true love. Pat, disguised as Dr. de Blinko, was very comical indeed.

Everybody was so pleased with the whole show that the C.O. asked for an encore performance, which was given on Boxing Night, when most of the village inhabitants were invited, and they seemed to have enjoyed the programme. In fact, this, with many other little friendly incidents, caused the Unit to be looked upon as sons of the village.

Taking into consideration the poor conditions under which we were then living, and that the Division Xmas truck was lost on its way up from the Base, this Xmas, if anything, excelled the prior one we enjoyed jointly at Poperinghe and Ypres.

J. A. SLADE.

THE R.A.M.C.

Have you heard of the work of the R.A.M.C. ?
A Corps you may sometimes hear slandered ;
Have you heard of their deeds at advanced R.A.P.
When the big German guns have a-thundered ?

" Meds " don't advertise, or put on any " side,"
When their errands of mercy pursuing—
The *Gazette* decorations to others are plied,
For the R.A.M.C. not much is doing !

But the Infantryman in a " stunt " or a " raid "
Knows perfectly well if he's wounded
The Red Cross Man quickly will render first-aid ;
His trust in his chum is well founded.

When Boche shells are bursting 'twixt front line and rear,
And most men in dug-outs are resting,
With stretcher on shoulder, and never a fear,
Go the bearers, though Death they are testing.

So when you are inclined to utter a sneer
At the Medical Corps when you see them,
Remember their great deeds in time will appear
In records which from slurs will free them.

DUNCAN M'CALLUM,
Herts. Redoubt,
19th March, 1918.

A LAMENT TO MY GREATCOAT.

Greatcoat of mine—eh, what are you for ?
You that I lug over kilos galore ;
You that are folded so often by me,
To go in my pack for a General to see.

Greatcoat of mine—what a nuisance you are,
When the end of a march can be seen from afar,
When the spire of the church first comes into view,
How soon I'd be there if it were not for you !

Greatcoat of mine—through the heat of the day,
When I'd much rather lie on a cart-load of hay,
I guess you're the cause of th' expression of views
In language I certainly never should use.

Greatcoat of mine—what a bother you are,
Each button must look a bright, shining star ;
All the mud you collect must be well brushed away,
There's a great big inspection on orders to-day.

And yet in the winter with wind, oh ! so cold,
I stand on parade as in those days of old
When the sun used to shine and the breezes were warm,
And we dream'd not nor thought of these days of storm.
You lie in a barn and are not to be worn,
While we stand and we shiver and look so forlorn,
For the orders have said you must always be laid
Folded, on bed during inspection parade !

H. STOCKER.

History of the Unit.

CHAPTER VI.

GIVENCHY—FESTUBERT, SPRING, 1918.

"Rest" was all too short, after the trying experiences of the last few months. So enjoyable was the time spent at Audincthun that two months soon passed way. On February 7th the Unit was on the march, in a deluge of wind and rain, towards more active surroundings. Cuhem lodged us that night, and the march was continued during the next day, billets being occupied at Busnes the following night. Annezin was reached on February 9th, and there the Hospital was opened in a school. On the 14th February the Unit entered Bethune to establish the M.D.S. at the College St. Vaast, where ample accommodation was available. At this time we cleared the Divisional front immediately south of the La Bassée Canal, and the A.D.S. was situated at "Harley Street."

On March 4th the College St. Vaast was vacated, and the Unit moved to Les Harrisoirs, near Locon. The front south of the La Bassée Canal was no longer cleared by us, but A.D.S.'s had now been established at Tuning Fork (a little to the east of Gorre) and Lone Farm (near Pont Fixe), and the evacuation of sick and wounded from the Givenchy-Festubert front was our work.

This front was warming up considerably, the shelling, both H.E. and gas, and the night aerial bombing telling the old tale. On March 30th the quiet country area of Les Harrisoirs was left for the College St. Vaast once more.

THE BATTLE OF BETHUNE.

AT HEADQUARTERS.

The morning of April 9th, 1918, will be one which will ever remain in the memory of all units of the 55th Division. The disposition of the Unit previous to the German attack was two advanced dressing stations (at Lone Farm and Tuning Fork), with Major F. Ellis and Major Watson-Williams respectively in charge, with the necessary staff for each post, plus a few bearers in reserve ; the two Brigades in the Line had four bearers attached to each of the six battalions, and one Brigade was in reserve. The Headquarters of the Unit was in the College St. Vaast, Béthune, a most commodious building used previous to the shelling of the town as a Casualty Clearing Station.

Though the Unit was clearing the forward area, all casualties were being evacuated direct to No. 1 C.S.S., Chocques, or No. 18 C.C.S., Lapugnoy. Sick were being evacuated to the 2/1st West Lancs. Field Ambulance. The Unit, however, was taking scabies and septic skin cases, and on the morning of the 8th April had about 50 cases in.

The enemy had been active for some time, and an attack was not unexpected. Dawn of the 9th broke very foggy, with no wind, and was ushered in by a very heavy bombardment from the enemy, rapidly accentuated by our own guns. The noise soon awoke every one at H.Q., and though no messages had been received from the A.D.S.'s, it was obvious that an attack was in progress. Reveille was therefore sounded, and breakfast issued at 6 a.m. Communication was attempted with the A.D.S.'s, but owing to the heavy barrage this was impossible. It was found, however, that the enemy had broken through on the Portuguese front and were advancing on Locon. The reserve Brigade had been thrown in to form a protective flank running from Festubert towards Locon, parallel with the La Bassée Canal. In order to deal with casualties on this front a third A.D.S. was opened at Le Hamel, under Lieut. Pearce.

A few walking casualties reached the H.Q. at Béthune between 7 a.m. and 8 a.m., and shortly after the first car from Tuning Fork got through. A Main Dressing Station was opened at H.Q., and from then onwards all casualties were collected there and evacuated to C.C.S. Information came from Lone Farm to say that Battersea Bridge was down, and that the Ambulance stationed there could not get across the Canal. Arrangements were made to evacuate by hand along the Canal bank to Le Preol, where a bridge was intact, and where a car rendezvous was formed. A steam launch was sent to Beuvry and made several trips between there and Béthune on the 9th and 10th, bringing down chiefly sitting cases. The evacuation by car from Tuning Fork was very difficult owing to the heavy barrage on Gorre, but thanks to the gallantry of the car-drivers and assistance from the 141st Field Ambulance, which had opened at Beuvry, that area was kept clear.

The Tuning Fork A.D.S. was found to be untenable owing to enemy shelling for some hours in the early afternoon, and the A.D.S. withdrew to Le Hamel, to again re-open about 5 p.m. A steady stream of casualties was now coming in to the M.D.S., but there being an ample supply of cars from the 12th M.A.C., it was kept clear. M.A.C. cars were pushed forward to clear the A.D.S.'s, and did

LABOURSE TUNNEL, JULY 1918.

splendid work during the action. Reports from the forward area showed no accumulation of wounded.

Throughout the night the work went steadily on at the M.D.S., in spite of several shells falling on the building, and an ample supply of shrapnel all round. The shelling in the forward area was the heaviest ever experienced, with a large amount of gas. This gas was aided by there being no wind, which allowed it to hang about, but thanks to the care exercised by all ranks in wearing respirators, the Unit had only one casualty from gas.

Additional bearers from the 2/1st West Lancs. Field Ambulance arrived during the evening of the 9th, and they were sent forward as required. Other bearers from the 1/3rd West Lancs. Field Ambulance arrived during the night.

The 10th was another dull, windless day. The enemy's fire was still intense, with much gas, especially so in the neighbourhood of Gorre and Le Hamel. Evacuations were now proceeding satisfactorily. Battersea Bridge was again passable for cars, which expedited the evacuations from that side of the Front. Owing to the road from Gorre to the Tuning Fork A.D.S. being badly shell-holed, the A.D.S. was withdrawn to Gorre Chateau, the evacuation to that point being done by a series of relay posts. An accumulation of wounded had occurred at Loisne Chateau, where Capt. Bell was established as temporary M.O. with the 1/5th South Lancs., the previous M.O. being Lieut. McNeil, who was wounded early on the 9th. Attempts were made from Le Hamel to get a car there, but the car was knocked out and the cases had to be relayed, a very trying experience for the bearers. The Le Hamel A.D.S. had a very bad day, being heavily shelled, and the road through Essars to Béthune was more than " warm."

The shelling of Béthune increased, and the M.D.S. was hit several times. About 5 p.m. a 15-inch shell drove in the front of the building occupied as a temporary billet by the Unit's transport, killing and wounding several.

Assistance for the M.D.S. work had arrived in the shape of the 2nd Field Ambulance, which came in during the morning, and which carried on the work during the night of the 10th-11th, giving our personnel a rest after being on from the early morning of the 9th. The dressing room and all patients were removed to the cellars of the buildings, which were fairly good for safety.

The night of the 10th-11th will long be remembered by those at the A.D.S. in Gorre Chateau. The Chateau, full of troops and wounded, more wounded lying out in the Chateau grounds on stretchers owing to lack of any cover, the continual whistle and roar of shells in the darkness of a night on which the angel of death was very near, gave memories which we shall never forget.

On the 11th it was thought advisable to send the transport and all Headquarters' personnel other than those required as reliefs for the forward area, further back, and they were dispatched to the C.C.S. site at Chocques, this Unit having moved.

Capt. Rogers, of the 1/3rd West Lancs. Field Ambulance, had relieved Lieut. Pearce at Le Hamel, and he very ably arranged a system of evacuation from Loisne Chateau.

Lieut. Pearce established a post at the junction of the Essars and Locon roads, where he collected casualties from the neighbouring batteries.

The night of the 11th-12th was quieter, apart from an increased shelling of Béthune.

On the 12th, it was decided to close the M.D.S. at Béthune and open at Chocques, where the transport had gone the preceding day. A party was left in Béthune to deal with any local casualties. The A.D.S. in Gorre Chateau was moved into Gorre Brewery, a building with good cellar protection.

The intensity of the action from now onwards commenced to die down. On the 15th, the A.D.S. at Le Hamel was closed, and on the 16th the A.D.S.'s at Gorre Brewery and Lone Farm were handed over on relief to the 1st Division.

No mere words can express the experience of the Unit from the 9th—16th April. It passed through the fire and covered itself with distinction. At no time during those days was there any congestion of wounded forward, for every Officer, N.C.O. and man was out to do his all, and did it to the satisfaction of those in authority, earning the highest praise. The fact that the Unit won in this action 1 Bar to D.S.O., 2 Bars to M.C., 1 M.C., 2 D.C.M.'s, 1 Bar to M.M., 6 M.M.'s, and 3 Croix de Guerre shows how highly we were appreciated, and to what a high standard the work rose in this action.

In a battle in which everyone did such excellent work, it is impossible to select individuals for special praise. Too much praise, however, cannot be given to the Motor Transport drivers and Orderlies, who ran the gauntlet of the barrage to get the wounded away from the front, or who amongst the falling buildings of Béthune rescued and carried away the wounded civilians.

It was a great battle. Long will it remain in the memories of those who endured it, and who may well feel proud of their work during those days.

W.B.

THE BATTLE OF BETHUNE.

IN THE LINE.

Early in February, 1918, the Division was ordered into the line, and occupied a position in front of La Bassée. This sector had remained almost unchanged since November, 1914, and was remarkable, to the eyes of those who had spent months at Ypres and on the Somme, for the small extent of destruction. The Ambulance almost immediately took over the entire evacuation, the main Dressing Station being located in Béthune itself, and two advanced dressing-stations, the right in a large isolated and strengthened farmhouse (Lone Farm), the left in an estaminet at Tuning Fork.

Although close to the line, civilian inhabitants remained in this last area, and retailed indifferent beer and fried potatoes at prices which justified the charge of profiteering. The comparative calm which had brooded over the district since the Battle of Festubert, in 1915, soon underwent a change ; and the civilians began to look upon the "Roses" with much disfavour as disturbers of the peace.

News of the big German attacks in the south caused a good deal of anxiety, especially as it seemed that the Germans had developed the new tactics of the Battle of Cambrai to our disadvantage. The sector which the Division held was the only shield to the last coal-mines remaining in French hands, and a big advance through Béthune would have been fraught with grave consequences, not only to the Division, but to the whole line.

Nothing of great moment occurred, however, until the ninth of April. On that date a bombardment of a ferocity never before seen was opened at 4-15 a.m. over a wide front embracing the whole of our sector, and that of several divisions to the north. About five a massed infantry attack was launched, and penetrated, without breaking, our front line.

On the right brigade front the fight raged round the low hill of Givenchy, sweeping on till the enemy troops reached a ditch about 200 yards in front of Lone Farm. Major Ellis was in command here, with Lieut. Morrison. His communications were cut by the breaking of the bridge over the La Bassée Canal early in the morning. About ten o'clock it seemed as though the attack would sweep right on over the A.D.S.

So rapid had been the advance that few casualties had come in, and these and the bulk of the personnel were ordered back along the north side of the Canal to the next bridge, Major Ellis and a small staff remaining. Before the move could be executed, however, the tide of the enemy advance appeared to stop. One German actually entered the courtyard of the farm, but before twelve o'clock the attack under vigorous local counter-attacks throughout the brigade area collapsed, and our line remained practically unchanged. There had been captured, however, two squads of bearers, at Windy Corner and at Queen's Road, (Ptes. L. G. Stoneman, killed ; E. H. Jones, G. Baxter, A. Walker, T. H. Lee, and R. S. Reynolds), and these had to be replaced, and the heavy task of clearing casualties of both sides undertaken. Although shelling was active all day, there were no special features, and the casualties were all removed.

On the front of the left Brigade all had not gone so well. The Portuguese Division to the North had completely collapsed at the first blow, and the enemy poured through, isolating and destroying the two British companies forming our flank. Fortunately, here as elsewhere, the thick mist augmented by a deluge of gas, caused the attack even more inconvenience than the defence, and the advance after the first two miles became disorganised and slowed down. The reserve Brigade, thrown in to form a defensive flank to the North, and facing N.E., was able to establish a line, while Divisional H.Q. was rapidly withdrawn from what had become the front line. The divisional position had to be held "at all costs," and the sharp salient thus created, with Festubert at its apex, was maintained.

At the A.D.S., where Major Watson-Williams was in command, with Capt. Robinson, the magnitude of the attack was apparent from the bombardment, of which—being just in front of several battery positions, with another in front again—we received a flattering proportion ! The actual dressing-station was being wrecked, and the casualties which came in, many of the gunners being among them, had to be dressed in the dug-out. Communication with the rear was impossible for cars till noon. About that time rifle bullets began to strike the buildings from the North. It was clear that the station was too far forward for the new state of affairs, and so it was withdrawn to Le Hamel, joining there an improvised station, organised by Lieut. Pearce, M.O.R.C., U.S.A.

In the late afternoon firing died down considerably, and it was then found possible to take a car right up behind Festubert. The clearing of casualties during the day was effected by means of prisoners, each four of whom passing down carried a stretcher. By nightfall all cases which had come in during the day were got away.

In the evening and again during the night fresh attacks were launched against us, and the next morning the line of evacuation through Le Hamel had to be abandoned. Cars managed to reach and clear the old A.D.S., and by seven o'clock on the 10th Gorre Chateau was organised as the new A.D.S. Bearers from 1/3rd W. Lancs. had come up during the night, and fresh and stronger relays were arranged throughout the left and centre Brigades.

The night of the 10th-11th will always remain a memory of horror. An intense bombardment of the whole area was maintained. Cars could not come up, and wounded poured in. The 13th K.L.R. were in Gorre, and suffered many casualties. Gorre Chateau and village were bombarded with 340 and 420 m.m. shells, which reduced to powder the whole area around their point of impact. Finally, about 4 a.m., cars began to come up under very heavy fire, and enjoying some miraculous escapes the whole of the wounded were again cleared.

The most wonderful bravery was shewn by both bearers and car drivers on the 9th and during this night, and their efforts in removing wounded under the most terrific fire deserve praise higher than it is possible for the written word to convey.

Early on the 11th the A.D.S. was moved to the cellars of Gorre Brewery. A contingent of the 2/1st W. Lancs. arrived, and it was possible to relieve the exhausted men. For the first time since the beginning of the battle it was possible also to visit the right A.D.S. and see how our men were faring there. They had been spared the second bombardment, and the A.D.S. itself had not suffered many hits during the first—in fact, an appearance of comparative peace existed, and the damage done had been in some measure already repaired.

The succeeding attacks on the divisional front, though fierce, were local, and mainly devoted to fruitless attempts of the enemy to take Festubert, the ruins of which covered the north flank of

"REPAIR FARM," JULY, 1918.

Givenchy Hill, as Givenchy Hill covered Béthune. No further events of exceptional interest occurred before the Ambulance was relieved by the 1st Division on the 16th, and the A.D.S. personnel with all the relays returned to Chocques, where all three ambulances were.

After eight days in reserve, chiefly devoted to marching, the Ambulance came to the new main dressing-station at Ruitz. Here events were peaceful enough, various rumours of impending attacks, and nightly air-raids alone breaking the monotony, if we except an inter-ambulance horse-show, which afforded much pleasant amusement. In June the Ambulance returned to its " normal position," and took charge of evacuations in the Division for the rest of the War. The A.D.S. was fixed at Labourse, with a small post at Repair Farm, while tunnelling in the bank at Labourse for a safer A.D.S. was begun. Nothing of interest occurred here, the summer being distinctly restful, which we much appreciated. The H.Q.'s were at Vaudricourt, and were not very comfortable. However, the Unit enjoyed a good deal of cricket there.

Towards the end of July the tunnel at Labourse was finished. In two days the transfer was to take place, when Major Ellis was most unluckily wounded by a splinter of shell while he was on the steps of the A.D.S.

E.W.W.

History of the Unit.

CHAPTER VII.

THE LAST PHASE.

Throughout July and August matters kept quiet and the Ambulance remained in the line. Towards the end of August, in connection with the Allied advance in the south, we began to press the enemy, and a series of small actions took place. Finally in September the Germans found the sector too hot for them. They shelled Vaudircourt on two occasions, and we lost some men who were wounded in their billet at night ; and when the Ambulance shortly after this moved to Béthune we were again shelled.

The German retreat now began in earnest and we hurried off behind them to hamper it. An entirely new phase of warfare commenced, and we soon pushed through the devastated area and got into country which had seen no fighting.

A very rapid advance entailed a hard march over roads which the enemy had carefully destroyed. The fighting, however, was not severe, and we were delayed only at the Scheldt. Here Esplechin lodged our headquarters, and Froidmont Asylum over A.D.S. In the latter place one of our men was wounded.

The work now was almost as much care of the civilian sick and wounded as of our own. In the next step of the advance on November 9th a shell dropped almost at the door of the A.D.S. at Tournai, killing Dvr. A. J. Deviell and Pte. R. D. W. Richardson, and wounding Capt. Robinson and Staff-Sergt. Gee.

We marched on over crowded roads—sometimes five columns abreast moved along—and got into Ath, where we established the first A.D.S. in that town early on the 11th. The whole town was en fete, and we had a very cheery reception. In the middle of the morning the Armistice was declared and the rejoicing redoubled.

The remainder of the story is only of amusements and moves. From Ath we moved to most luxurious billets near Brussels at the beginning of December. Dances and football occupied much of our ample leisure, and the beautiful but expensive city of Brussels was always within our reach.

The Christmas celebrations lacked one feature—the presence of Lieut.-Col. Blackwood, who had commanded the unit so successfully since July, 1917, and who was summoned home on December 14th, as his patients there could no longer spare him. He had covered himself with glory during the year and a half he was in command, and the Ambulance under him won a position and reputation which was without peer in the Division. We all deplored very sincerely the parting with a brave and trusted leader.

Before leaving us, Lieut.-Col. Blackwood was instrumental in founding the 2/1st Wessex Field Ambulance Comrades' Association, a branch of the 55th Division Association.

The end of 1918 finds everyone with his attention concentrated on demobilisation and the anticipated early return to that civil life from which we have all so long been strangers. Though we all express ourselves as anxious only for this, it cannot be without very heartfelt regret that we turn our backs on the Army and the Ambulance that for four years has been our home. Only the certainty that we shall have many opportunities for meeting and for recalling the dangers, the hardships, and the enjoyment which we have all shared can mitigate this feeling. A second line unit, we cannot hope to survive the demobilisation, and as each man is '' dismissed '' for the last time, the history of the 2/1st Wessex Field Ambulance comes to an end.

E.W.W.

An Evening with the Wessex Sergeants.

I shall niver ferget wan day in France I 'appened to rin up 'gainst an ole friend of mine—Sam Bart he's name was, and he lives at a place called Teignmouth. He axed me to come auver to hes place to see he's 'osses—he was a turrible chap 'bout 'osses, an' wat he did'n knaw 'bout 'em wad'n worth knawing—an' he sed I shude be plaised to see some of he's friend from Demshur, an' 'ave a little chat way 'em an' a sing-song.

Seein' I be a Deb'n chap mezel, I thought twude be a bit of a change, so I goes long way un, an' arter I'd 'ad a gude look at he's 'osses, he axed me to come in the Sergeants' Mess, where all he's friends was.

'Twas a little shanty way two tables an' some vorms, an' round the tables there was a lot of young fellers, purty nigh twenty I shude think.

They 'ad just finished tay, an' they was chitterin' like a lot of jack-daws. I had a cup of tay arter I'd bin interduced to all o'm. They was a rare lot o' chaps, an' it seemed like ole times to 'ear a bit of the ole' Deb'n.

Arter a little while, wan o'm sed, "Who's gwain to twist 'em up?"—I did'n knaw what that meant, but sivver o'm, most o'm in fac', seated theirsels roun' wan table, an' started playin' way a pack o' cards. I dunnaw whe'er I kin remember the names of all o'm, but there was Bill—I fancy he was the ringleader—Archie, Len, Sid, Harry, Albert, Charley, Jack, Frank, Alec an' Claude.

Well, Bill 'ad the cards, an' he 'ad he's coat off, an' was swattin' like a bull. He giv'd a card to each wan o'm, an' arter they'd looked at 'n they put some money down. Wan wude put a penny, anuther tuppence, an' wan or two o' the more reckless wans, like Charley and Claude, wude put a shillin'. Bill wude keep a card fer e'sel, an' then e'd give 'em anuther card all roun'.

Then sumbody wude say "Twist," an' he'd giv'm anuther card. Anuther wude say "Appy" an' he wud'n git wan. Anuther wude say "Bust it." He'd 'ave anuther card, an' by the explosion that followed I shude think sumthin' DID bust!—Then Bill wude turn up he's awn cards, an' they that 'ad more'n he 'ad got some money, an' they wat 'ad less los' their money. W'en Bill 'ad 'ad a gude turn somebody else wude 'ave a go, an' so it went awn.

I axed Sam w'at they called they was playin' an' he sed 'twas called "Pontune." I'd niver seed the game bevore, an' I daun reckon much o't. I'd soonder play "Snap" mezel.

There was only two or dree at the other table. Wan o'm—Alfy he's name was—was bizzy writin' letters. He was a daddy fer writin' letters, be wot I cude yer. Use to write dree or vower ivry day.

Then there was anuther oldish chap, called Jack, playin' way a pack o' cards all to e'sel. Anuther chap called "Trinny" was writin' down in a buke 'ow many miles he's motos had done, an' 'ow much oil he'd used. Anuther wan, called George, was tryin' to fin' the best way to git "up the line," cuz he was gwain there the next' mornin' way the C.O.

Well, twad'n long bevore 'twas supper time an' us all sat down to a cup o' tay, and bit of bread'n-cheese. They was chitterin' all the time, 'bout all sorts o' subjects till wan o'm—Frank I bleeve 'twas—sed that Bidevord 'ad more men in the Army an' Navy than any other town in England.

My eyes! but you shude 'ave 'eard the uproar! Everybody started shoutin' to wance, an' I thought Frank was in fer a rough time. Wan wude stick up fer Dawlish, anuther fer Teignmouth, an' anuther fer Ex'ter, till I thought my 'aid would a got addled. The 'Ouse of Parli'ment, or even a mother's meetin' wad'n in it. Then Frank sed that if Bidevord 'ad'n more men in the Army an' Navy than any other town in England, it 'ad the bes' market in the world, an' then the fat was in the vire again, an' the row was wuss than ever. I bleeve Frank was only 'aving a game way 'em, but I 'ardly knawed wot to make o't.

They quieted down arter a bit, and then my fren' Sam suggested us finish up way a little 'armony. So us 'ad a bit of a sing-song, an' I mus' say I enjoyed it. They 'ad some rare singers there, sure 'nuff, and they singed some very purty songs. I was sorry w'en they finished, but 'twas gittin' late now, an' time fer me to be makin' tracks fer 'ome. So I wished 'em all gude night, an' sed I 'oped I shude meet 'em all again some day, an' now that the 'ole war is auver, I 'ope I shall soon be seeing most, if not all o'm, in dear ole' Demshur.

UNCLE TOM COBLEIGH.
(J.H.)

Christmas, 1918.

This glorious Xmastide was spent by all ranks of the " Wessex " with gay and happy hearts, for the grim toil and strife on the shell-torn battlefield lay far behind us, and a victory of Right over Might had at last crowned all our efforts. What a difference in conditions to prior Xmas times out there !

All had really first-class billets, in a select residential suburb of Brussels. The people took every man to their hearts and were bent on giving all a jolly good time. A splendid hall was placed at our disposal, and here, on Xmas Eve, the boys indulged in a Dance. Numerous civilian friends were invited, and hopped round in great style. Credit is due to the Dance Committee for the excellent arrangements.

The Xmas dinner, as usual, was first-class, and the cooks, all of whom were experts at their job by this time, and the Quartermaster's Department deserved every praise for their efforts to give the lads a treat.

After dinner, the O.C., Major A. J. D. Riddett, proposed the toast " To absent Comrades," and this was drunk in silence. It was certain that everyone's thoughts went back to the old pals who had marched into " Action " with us, and who had given their lives that others might live. Ah ! we can see them now, the happy, lighthearted fellows, some of the finest that ever left old England's shores.

Unfortunately the Unit had not been settled long enough for the Concert Party to get going, so there was no concert provided. The majority of the Unit had invitations from civilian friends for the evening. The few who did not spent a pleasant social evening in the Recreation Room. As the anniversary of the Unit's landing in France, the 14th January, drew nigh, it was decided to celebrate the occasion in royal style.

J. A. SLADE.

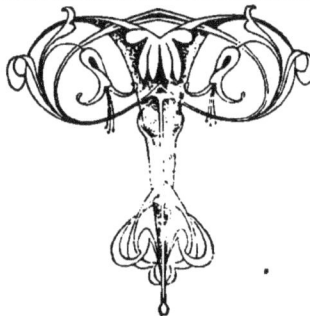

History of the Unit.

CHAPTER VIII.

(By H. R. Rand).

Wonderful is the trait in man, that of forgetting the unpleasant and remembering only the happy incidents of the many which make any particular epoch in life memorable. The memories of the Great War will be with us in the future, and we shall spend many a pleasant evening of reminiscence with our homefolk. Many thoughts, of course, will centre round the closing event of our Active Service career, the stay in Espinette, a few miles from Brussels.

On arrival as Espinette, dead-beat after a very trying march, we were detailed in parties for our billets, which were all in private houses, and many of us had beds and every convenience that helps to make life pleasant. We were very kindly received by our hosts, who did all that friends could do to make our stay with them enjoyable. It need hardly be said that after the rough experiences of three years, sleeping in huts, barns, under canvas, and in any other place where men could be billetted thirty or forty together, the new conditions were more than appreciated. An ideal recreation room was found in the large room of the " Prince d'Orange," a popular café well known to the enthusiastic supporters of the " Vivier d'Oie " Football Club. Many a happy time was spent in this room, perhaps the most memorable ones being the dance on Christmas Eve, the Christmas dinner, and the dance on New Year's Eve. Who will forget one item in the latter dance—that never-to-be-forgotten Twilight Waltz, so full of reminiscences of kissing episodes for many?

The third anniversary of the Unit's landing in France was celebrated in great style on the 14th January, 1919. The Officers gave a dinner at 4-30 p.m., followed by a concert by artists from the 166th Brigade. Later in the evening our own inimitable Sketch Party gave a " show," which was well appreciated, " Pat's " wonderful " Woodland Fairies " being the star turn, in which our great artiste, Mr. Cecil Ireland, excelled himself.

Brussels had great claims on our attention, and many visits of combined education and pleasure were paid to that fine city, of great significance to the Allies as the capital of unconquerable Belgium, and the home of Albert, its gallant King, the spirit of Belgium personified. Brussels possesses all the attractions of an ideal city in buildings, both ancient and modern—among them being the "Palais de Justice," the " Palais Royale," the " Hotel de Ville," and " le Maison du Roi." Happy crowds thronged the Boulevardes, so pleased were they to have seen the last of the arrogant enemy, and to show their appreciation of Britain's part in his overthrow by their cordial friendship.

Brussels has numerous places of amusement, theatres, cinemas, a skating rink, etc., all catering for various tastes. Parties, under an able guide, Major Watson-Williams, were given the opportunity of visiting the " Hotel de Ville," and seeing many fine rooms not open in the ordinary way, including that of Burgomaster Max, the Council Chamber, and the Registrar's Office. These rooms contain many objects of interest, and some remarkable tapestries picturing historic events. The Art Museum was also visited. It contains a valuable collection of sculptures and pictures, many of the latter by such celebrated old masters as Reubens and Rembrandt. The Museum Wertz was found very interesting with its collection of paintings by the artist of that name. Music-lovers found a great source of pleasure at the " Theatre Royal de la Monnaie," and listened with delight to such operas as " La Fille du Regiment," " La Boheme," and " Faust."

It is said that one's visit to Brussels is incomplete without having seen the historic battlefield of Waterloo, so parties under the guidance of Major Watson-Williams and Capt. Bell journeyed to Waterloo and saw all that thousands of tourists from all directions had seen during the last hundred years. As one who had taken part in the overthrow of modern militarism viewed this significant scene in the history of England, where previously a similar deed had been accomplished, one felt justly proud that on both occasions men of our race had fought and died for the highest ideals of mankind.

Sportsmen had ample opportunities of enjoying the favourite pastimes, football—Association and Rugby—easily being the most popular. The Belgians had several clever teams and provided many fine games. Our Allies gave exhibitions of the finest football seen by the '' Wessex '' whilst on active service.

A WELL-KNOWN SCENE.

January 3rd, 1919, was a memorable day in the Division's history, being the third anniversary of its formation and of joining the B.E.F., and the occasion of a Review by the King of the Belgians, an honour which was keenly appreciated. The occasion was welcomed, because all admired the gallant King and the noble part played by him in the World War. All ranks were proud of the Division's services and of the great soldier in command.

Previously the following '' Special Order of the Day '' was presented to all :—

IN THE FIELD,

3rd January, 1919.

SOLDIERS OF THE 55TH DIVISION,

To-day is the third anniversary of the formation of your Division in France. With the exception of short periods of rest amounting to about four months in all, the Division has been in active daily touch with the enemy throughout these last three years, until the conclusion of the Armistice. During the whole of that time it has been my great privilege to command it. So to-day I want to give a message to every soldier, of all ranks, now with the Division, and through them to everyone of the sixty thousand who have served in it, and are still living.

Many, I am glad to say, who saw the formation of the Division are with us now, but very many more, who were serving then in the Division or who have served since, are not. There are some still suffering from wounds, and some whose graves we have left on hard-fought fields and behind grim trench-lines where they faced the enemy with such splendid courage and determination. They are not forgotten.

The Battles of the SOMME, YPRES, CAMBRAI and GIVENCHY-FESTUBERT took heavy toll of the Division, and the long wearisome trench warfare was not less costly. But every battle, and all the days of trench fighting, showed more and more clearly as time went on the stuff of which the Division was made, and enabled it to establish and maintain the proud reputation which now belongs to it.

We have gone through hard and anxious times together. Yet, however dim and far-off ultimate victory seemed, you never faltered or lost heart, you showed the same stubbornness in defence as you have shown boldness in attack. There was a time when things seemed almost desperate ; when we were forced by weight of numbers to await day after day fierce attack by a confident and relentless enemy. You knew how things were ; knew that, as the Field Marshal Commanding-in-Chief said in his Order of the Day, you stood with your backs to the wall ; but this knowledge only added to your dogged determination,—and you won through. The glorious victory you gained in the fighting from the 9th to the 16th April, 1918, when, outnumbered and with your flank turned, you withstood for days, without yielding ground, a series of violent attacks by an enemy already flushed with success, and, taking advantage of every opportunity for the offensive, inflicted on him the severest losses, was the first bright spot after many dark days. You may fairly claim to have left on him a mark that he carried to the end, and to have done your full share towards his ultimate destruction. It is believed that the front held by the Division was the only piece of the Allied Front, which, being attacked in force during the German offensive of 1918, was held to the end inviolate.

All commanders and staffs, all arms of services, and all ranks have played their part equally loyally. I want to thank you all for what you have done, to tell you how highly I value the support and trust you have always given me, and how intensely proud I am to have commanded such a Division in such a war.

What has stood us in the greatest stead throughout has been the magnificent spirit of comradeship that has run all through the Division, so that everyone has played up, not for himself, but with complete unselfishness for the good of the side, and with complete trust in his comrades. Such comradeship is the foundation and essence of true discipline.

Another great asset has been the unfailing cheerfulness with which dangers and hardships have been faced. I have never found a man of the Division who had not a smile ready, even in the blackest times.

Courage, determination, endurance, cheerfulness, unselfishness, these are the virtues that have pulled you through, and brought us victory at last.

Peace, we believe, will now soon be firmly established, and then we shall all be scattered. But wherever we go I hope we shall all still feel that we belong to the 55th Division, and shall retain the spirit that has made it what it is. You all know of the 55th Division Comrades' Association which has been formed. Its object is to keep in peace the spirit of comradeship which has bound us together in the face of the enemy, and to enable us to stand by each other in the future as we have in the past. I hope you will all join it.

As, owing to the manner in which demobilization is to be carried out, I may not have another opportunity, I wish everyone now in the Division, or who has been in it, success and happiness in whatever he may undertake.

H. S. JEUDWINE,
Major General,
COMMANDING 55TH (WEST LANCASHIRE) DIVISION.

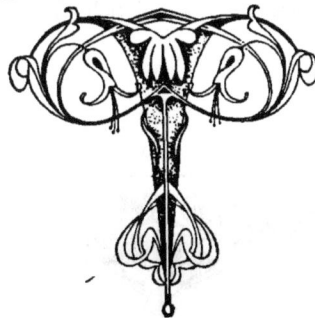

Our " Comrades' Association."

We feel that our Book would not be complete without some mention of the 2/1st Wessex Field Ambulance Comrades' Association which has been formed as a branch of the 55th Division Comrades' Association.

The aims are :—

(1) To perpetuate the splendid spirit of comradeship which characterised all ranks in the Unit while on Active Service.

(2) To promote and safeguard the interests of all who have served with us.

(3) To perpetuate the memory of our gallant comrades who made the great sacrifice, and to promote the welfare of their dependents.

(4) To observe anniversaries of great events in the history of the Unit, and to arrange social re-unions of its members .

The following officers have been elected :—President and Treasurer, Lieut.-Col. W. Blackwood, D.S.O.; Secretary, Sergt. W. Pearce ; Committee, Capt. G. W. Robinson, Sergt. H. Doidge (Exeter), Lce.-Corpl. R. D. McMaster (South Molton), Ptes. H. Taylor (Bradford), E. H. Wynn (Birkenhead), W. H. Beer (Tiverton), and H. Sellers (Penzance).

The subscription is one shilling per year.

Any men of the Ambulance desirous of joining the Association or obtaining information about it should communicate with Mr. W. Pearce, Council Schools, Kingsteignton, Devon.

www.ingramcontent.com/pod-product-compliance
Lightning Source LLC
Chambersburg PA
CBHW081141090426
42736CB00018B/3443

* 9 7 8 1 7 8 3 3 1 4 4 1 6 *